Becoming an Achiever

A Student Guide

By Carolyn Coil

Pieces of
Learning

© 2004 Pieces of Learning
CLC0344
ISBN 978-1-931334-57-0

www.piecesoflearning.com

Printed in the U.S.A.

Table of Contents

To

All of the students who use this book and become achievers

And

The parents, teachers, and other adults who work with them

And

Mona Livermont, my incredible typist!

From the Publisher

This book is for the student who wants to become an achiever. Both the narrative and the forms are an important part of the process. Over a period of time, a certain section will be important to the reader. The author asks the reader to reread the book sections again. Therefore, we ask that teachers and counselors honor the copyright laws.

Introduction

Thoughts on Becoming an Achiever

"Another 'D' … I hate math tests! My life would be a lot better without any schoolwork at all."

" My parents want me to be on the honor roll. I'd like that, too, but that means work. It means carrying books home and writing papers and doing my homework. It means memorizing a lot of stuff I think is boring. Is it really worth it?"

"People are starting to ask me what I want to do when I finish high school, where I want to go to college, and what career I want to have. To tell you the truth, I just want to be rich and have an expensive car. The way to do that is to win the lottery!"

"I used to brag about the fact that I got good grades on my tests, and I never studied. And that was true. In elementary school, I already knew all the things they were teaching us. I didn't even have to pay attention. But now…I should study, but I don't know how."

"Sometimes I pretend that I'm not smart at all. If I get a good grade and a boy asks me about it, I just say, 'Oh I didn't do very well.' I don't want the boys to think I'm smarter than they are. Then I wouldn't be very popular."

"I really want to do well in school, but my family doesn't think education is that important. When I get home from school, I have to cook dinner and look after all my little brothers and sister. My dad says school is a waste of time. He is looking forward to my sixteenth birthday because then I can quit school and get a full time job."

All of those quotes come from real kids – kids who are discouraged about school, kids who don't like to study, kids who want to be popular rather than brainy, kids whose parents don't see the value of getting a good education. Each one's story is a little different, but they all have one thing in common. They are all intelligent students like you who could do well and be high achievers in school.

You might be something like one of these kids. You may be really smart, but you're not doing very well in school. Some of your teachers may have called you an "underachiever." That means you are a student who has the ability to do better than you are doing. You may have gotten back an assignment or a test paper where the teacher has written, *"You could do better."* If any of these situations describe you, and if you think you could do better, then this book is for you.

Becoming an Achiever How is it Done?

You probably know kids in your class or your school who seem to succeed at everything. They always get A's, always know the answers in class, and always get the awards at the end of the school year.

Not everyone can succeed at everything, but everyone can become an achiever! There are no secret formulas. It takes some work on your part. The choice is yours. But if you are willing to try, this book will show you how.

THEN THE CHOICE TO TRY IS YOURS.

These are the topics
you will explore
as you read,
think,
and write about
Becoming an Achiever.

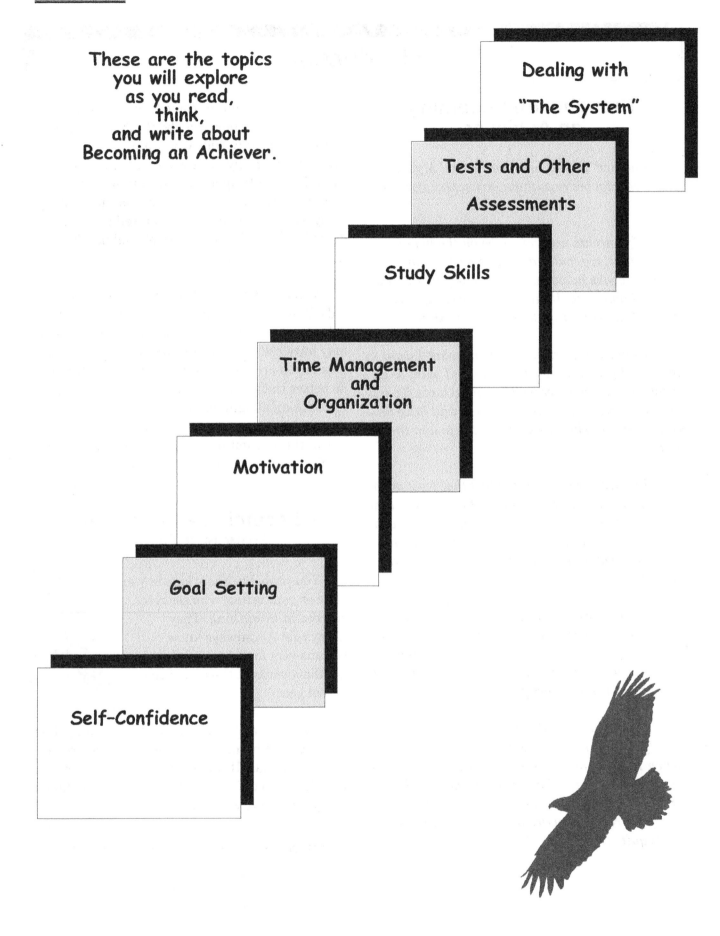

Dealing with

"The System"

Tests and Other

Assessments

Study Skills

Time Management
and
Organization

Motivation

Goal Setting

Self-Confidence

7 Steps to Success

1. Self-Confidence

Self-confidence *is a belief you have that you possess good qualities that are valuable to yourself and others.*

Did you ever stop to think that the person you need most to like you is YOU? If you don't like yourself very much, no one else will like you either. Liking oneself sometimes isn't easy, even for adults, but it is very important to have self-confidence that comes from the heart.

Self-confidence comes when you like yourself; and you realize you can use your strengths; and you can work to improve your weaknesses in order to affect what happens in your life.

You may never have thought about all of the good qualities you possess. It's much easier for most of us to recognize our own weaknesses. However, successful people usually know their strengths and weaknesses and learn to make the best of the talents they have. The first chapter in this book shows you **how to take a realistic look at both your good points and your bad points.** Then you'll see what you can do to make the good even better and what you can do to eliminate or change some of your weaknesses.

2. Goal Setting

Goal setting *is deciding on basic plans for your life that you will strive to achieve.* It's hard to know **if** you are achieving if you don't know

what you want to achieve. That's how many people go through life when they have no goals. An ancient proverb states:

> I CAN'T CONTROL
> THE WIND,
> BUT I CAN CONTROL
> THE WAY I SET MY SAILS

Think of a sailboat with its sails down, adrift on the ocean. Part of the journey may be relaxing and wonderful, but if you really want to get somewhere, you have to hoist the sails, set the rudder, and head in a planned direction. Learning how to set goals for your life is much like learning how to take control of the sailboat.

And setting goals for yourself is much like setting your sails. Most achievers set goals for themselves regularly, for goals act as the blueprint for what they do in their lives. This chapter shows you **how to set goals and take action** — to map out your life's blueprint and set your sails.

3. Motivation

Motivation *is the desire to do something.* We're all motivated to do many things. When you're hungry, you're motivated to go to the refrigerator and get something to eat or maybe to put a bag of popcorn into the microwave. Some motivations, like hunger, are very basic. Other types of motivation require a bit more maturity.

It's more difficult to motivate yourself to open your history book and study the chapter when your favorite TV show is on! It's more difficult to motivate yourself to learn your vocabulary words when you'd rather talk on the phone. It's more difficult to motivate yourself to struggle through your math homework when you could be playing a computer game!

You have to **want** to become an achiever. Motivation is important in becoming an achiever. Self-motivation is the hardest of all. You may have some people in your life who are outside motivators. They nag . . . oops, I mean help . . . you to get motivated. If you do, be thankful for them. They are helping you to become an achiever. The motivation section of this book shows you how to work with people who want to help you, but more importantly shows you **how to motivate yourself.**

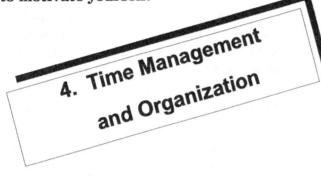

Organizing all your notes, notebooks, papers, and books to study for a test or to plan a project takes both effort and time, but it will pay off in the long run as you become a better student. How? **Being organized helps you make better use of your time.** Keeping your room and your belongings in order probably is something your parents have talked to you about, but did you know that learning this skill will also help you to become an achiever? So will learning how to use time management tools such as a calendar and a "To Do" list, because they help you plan the best uses for your time.

Being organized and learning how to schedule and manage your time are skills you need to learn – just like the skills you learned in reading and math. And, just like reading and math, these are skills you can use your whole life! The organization and time management chapter shows you **how to organize yourself and plan your time well** as you strive to become an achiever.

Studying is hard work! Many kids in American schools seem unwilling to put forth the effort that studying requires. Don't put yourself in that category. Forget being lazy! Make a commitment to do what it takes to develop the study skills you need.

The study skills chapter shows you **how to better listen in class, take notes, memorize information, and develop research skills.** You'll also learn the importance of discovering which academic skills you should have learned (but never did) and what to do about it. These things may seem a little boring to you, but they are worth knowing if you've made the decision to become an achiever. They are the tools you need to become an achiever. Many students who decide they really want to do well in school have no idea how to study. These students quickly lose their motivation when their grades remain low even though they are doing their best. With good study skills, this won't happen to you.

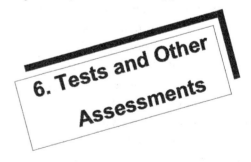

Knowing how to successfully take tests is a big part of becoming an achiever in today's schools. Part of being a good test taker is knowing the information. The other part is in mastering the skills of test taking. This chapter gives you many **helpful hints about how to take tests**. It shows you how to deal with test anxiety and how to analyze questions and plan responses.

You may also encounter other product and performance assessments. Teachers generally use these assessments for projects, writing assignments and other assignments where there is no right or wrong answer. **Rubrics** *can* give you and the teacher guidelines for assessing the quality of your work. Achievers pay attention to rubrics and read and follow them carefully.

Look at both test taking and your ability to use rubrics as you go through this chapter.

All of us, kids and adults, have to do some things just because the system requires it. It's better for you in the long run to follow the rules. Why? Because while you are trying to understand the system, you can investigate ways to change how the system is organized. The chapter entitled *Dealing with "The System"* will give you some **guidelines for understanding and maybe for helping to change the System.**

7. Dealing with "The System"

School, like the government, the military, business, and industry, is a "system." You may have heard your school district referred to as the "school system." **All systems have rules and regulations that everyone has to follow in order for the system to run smoothly for the majority of its people.** Organizations make rules so that they run smoothly. Unfortunately, sometimes these rules seem pretty senseless, and some students don't understand why they have to follow them.

Sometimes a teacher may ask you to do an assignment about information you already know. That seems senseless, but often that's just the way the system works. Some students say they won't do their assignments because the work is too boring or because they already know the answers and don't think they should have to write them down. These students are not achievers in school. It's not because they are dumb. It's because they refuse to follow the rules of "the system."

BECOMING AN ACHIEVER DOESN'T HAPPEN OVERNIGHT

How to Use This Book

To Read . . .

This book is for anyone who has decided to become an achiever but is not sure exactly how to do it. It has seven chapters, one chapter for each of the seven Steps to Success shown on page 6. It includes many stories about real kids so that you can understand some of the problems and successes that happen to kids as they work on becoming achievers. You might read this book by yourself. Or you might read it with your class. Either way, you may want to discuss the ideas in the book and your opinions with both your friends and classmates and with an adult. There are pages you may want to read again later when you find they are particularly important to you.

To Think and Reflect and Write . . .

You also have the opportunity to think about yourself and your own life. When you see the light bulb, and the words . . .

"Think About It!"

this means it is time to think about yourself and how what you've read or discussed applies to your own situation. Then write responses.

To Do . . .

this book has some pages that you may want to use over and over again. When you see the words . . .

Reproducible pages for student use . .

this means that you can copy the page so you can use it more than once.

If you read this book carefully, complete the questions, and try the suggestions, you will most certainly be on the road to becoming an achiever!

YES, YOU CAN!

1. Self-Confidence

"The art teacher came to our first grade classroom once a week. My first memory of doing something in art was a picture we were to draw of water, a tree, clouds, and the sun. This teacher wanted our picture to look 'just like' hers. I was overjoyed at the prospect of using a paintbrush and paints! But the art teacher hated my painting. She held it up to the entire class as an example of how not to paint. I was so embarrassed I wanted to die. I hated art and thought of myself as a failure in art for a long time."

You might think a fifth or sixth grader told that story. After all, it is a story about something that happened in first grade, and the person is remembering back. Actually, it is a teacher's story, and it had happened to her more than 50 years ago!

The story tells a little bit about self-confidence. Self-confidence doesn't come only from our ability to do things. It also comes from how good we feel about ourselves based on what **other** people have told us. The things other people say about us can be very powerful messages. In this story, the message was so powerful that the teacher remembered it 50 years! When asked what else she remembered about first grade, she couldn't remember a thing! The art teacher really made a negative impression on her and weakened her self-confidence.

Positive messages about ourselves work in the same way. Consider this story:

Susan is an eighth grader. She never thought that science was her best subject, but her science teacher seemed to think so. When they started discussing science projects, Susan wasn't too thrilled. She had never done a good project like some of the "scientific geniuses" in the school. But her teacher encouraged her to do some ecological experiments with plants. Susan enjoyed working outside and her teacher kept encouraging her, telling her she was making good progress and giving her suggestions that really made sense.

At the school science fair, Susan received a second place ribbon. Her teacher was proud, her parents were proud, and Susan felt good about herself. She feels more confident about science and thinks she may be an achiever in high school science classes after all.

These examples involve teachers and show how they can help or hurt a student's self-confidence. There are 3 categories of people who influence how you feel about yourself and your abilities.

Parents

Some kids have parents who think their children are wonderful. These parents encourage their children and praise everything they do. Other kids may have parents who are overly critical, who think that everything has to be perfect, or think that nothing their children do is right. There are also parents who are just too busy or too tired to pay much attention to their children. Most parents are combinations of these descriptions. Sometimes they think you are wonderful, sometimes they complain about everything you do, and sometimes they're too wrapped up in their own lives to really pay attention.

Think About It!

Think about your relationship with your parents.
Write down one time when one or both of them were proud
of you and really boosted your self-confidence.

When I got an A on my science test that
I had studied so hard for.

Write down one time when one or both of them were too critical or too busy
and your self-confidence went downhill.

When my mom was at her desk working
and wouldn't let me ask her a question.

You might want to show your parent or parents what you wrote or talk to
them about it. Did they know how important the situation was to you when
they boosted your self-confidence? Did they remember the situation? And
did they know how you felt when they were too critical or too busy? Did you
tell them? If not, why not?

Independence & Responsibility

Parents to the Rescue?

Some students think the best way to be an achiever is to have their parents take on all of the responsibility for them. For example, if you need a book for tonight's homework and left it at school, you may think it is up to your mom to hop in the car and get it. Otherwise, you won't finish your homework. Or perhaps you leave your lunch money on the kitchen table. The first thing you think of when you get to school is calling your dad to bring it to you.

While the 'parents-to-the-rescue' syndrome can bail you out of a short-term problem, it is not a very good strategy for a long-term solution. Many students use their parents in this way all through school and then are surprised when they get to college that there is no one there to take the responsibility for them.

Responsibility and independence go hand-in-hand. The more independence you have, the more responsibility should also be yours. Finding ways to be both independent and responsible is one of the best strategies for increasing your self-confidence as you become an achiever.

Think About It!

List the areas in your life where you have lots of independence.

dressing myself

List the areas in your life where you take on lots of responsibility.

school work + tennis

In which areas of your life are your parents still coming to the rescue for you?

making dinner/breakfast/lunch, running the laundary machine

List ways you could take on both more independence and more responsibility in these areas.

once a week I could try to make one of my meals

When You and Your Parents are New Immigrants

Some students have difficulty feeling self-confident when they and their parents are newly arrived immigrants to this country. If this is your situation, it is true that you face some special challenges. You may not understand how school works. You may not realize what the school expectations are or what the grading system is like. You may feel you have few friends and may believe that everyone knows more than you do. Your parents are probably feeling as confused as you are!

If your first language is not English, you have the additional challenge of learning not only the subject matter but learning a new language as well. All of this may seem confusing and overwhelming during the first few months in a new school. The good news is that as you come to study your new language and as you come to understand how school works, you are building the study skills, motivation, and attitudes everyone needs for school success. Ultimately, your persistence and hard work will pay off if you are willing to make the effort.

Most likely, you will catch on to American language and customs more rapidly than your parents will. This may put you in the position of teaching them some of what you are learning. Be patient with them, and try to explain new things in ways they will understand. Success in this endeavor will most definitely boost your self-confidence and should boost theirs as well!

Think About It!

If you are new to this country, what puzzles you most about school?

Language Arts would be hard

How can you deal with these concerns?

get a tutor or study a lot

How can you best help your parents adjust to their new country?

help them with things around the house

If you are NOT a new immigrant, how can you help students new to your school and new to this country feel accepted and welcomed?

talk to them or sit with them at lunch

Other Family Members

Your parents aren't the only ones in your family who may affect your self-confidence. If you have brothers, sisters, stepbrothers, stepsisters, grandparents, or others living in your household, they can be a big factor affecting how you feel about yourself.

Sometimes your brothers, sisters, and other family members are terrific. They help you out when you need them, stick up for you when someone is trying to put you down, and point out all of your good qualities when you feel like you're a nobody.

Sometimes, though, brothers and sisters aren't quite so kind. They know all of your bad points and are the first ones to point them out to you. You may think they are bigger, or smarter, or cuter, or tougher, or more talented than you are. You may feel that your parents always take their side of the story, always give them more, and always let them do the things they don't allow you to do. Many kids lose their self-confidence because of something their brother or sister has said or done.

Think About It!

What are some things that your brother, sister, or other family member has done that made you feel good about yourself?

Told me how great I was

What feelings did you have? Did you tell them? They might not be aware of how you felt.

I felt good about myself

What are some things they have said or done that have made you lose confidence in yourself? Told me I have done something inccorectly

What feelings did you have? Did you tell them? If not, why not? It might be good for them to know what makes you feel bad.

It made me feel like I haven't accomplished anything

Teachers

On the first page of this chapter were two stories about teachers and how their words affected two different students. If you were thinking about your own life when you read those two stories, you probably could think of teachers who have affected you in much the same way.

Just like any other group of adults, there are some teachers who are more positive and more enjoyable to be around than are others. Some teachers encourage you and make you feel good about yourself, even when you aren't doing too well with your schoolwork. Other teachers may make you feel that no matter what you do, it will be wrong, and they won't like it.

Students who are achievers realize that they won't always please all of their teachers, but they will try to do their best anyway. Other students lose their self-confidence when a teacher is negative, and they feel they will be a failure no matter what they do. Then they give up and stop trying.

If you feel like giving up, right now is the time to put your **gears in reverse and head in the opposite direction!**

Think About It!

Write down three positive things about yourself that teachers or other adults have told you.

- good job
- correct
- nice try

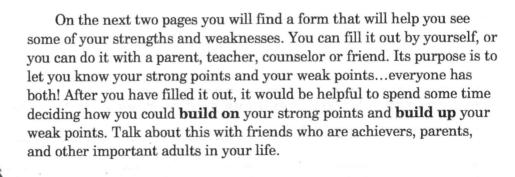

Notice that no one is asking you to write down the negative things about yourself that you have heard over the years. Unfortunately, most people remember these much longer than they should without ever writing them down!

On the next two pages you will find a form that will help you see some of your strengths and weaknesses. You can fill it out by yourself, or you can do it with a parent, teacher, counselor or friend. Its purpose is to let you know your strong points and your weak points...everyone has both! After you have filled it out, it would be helpful to spend some time deciding how you could **build on** your strong points and **build up** your weak points. Talk about this with friends who are achievers, parents, and other important adults in your life.

Personal Characteristics of Students
Who Are Becoming Achievers...

Rate yourself in these areas. First, mark a check under **S** for all those items that indicate your strengths. Next, count the number of strengths you have checked. Then check **W** for weaknesses; BUT you are not allowed to check more weaknesses than strengths.

S	W	
✓	___	I have confidence in myself.
✓	___	I let my teachers know when I am having a problem and work with them in problem solving.
___	✓	I am a risk-taker.
✓	___	I am willing to work to make changes in myself.
✓	___	I listen to those in authority over me.
___	✓	I take responsibility for my problems and do not put all of the blame on others.
✓	___	I work well in a group that is working on a constructive project.
✓	___	I have a close friend or friends who share similar positive interests.
___	✓	I am flexible and can see more than one possible solution when solving a problem.
✓	___	I have an area of special interest.
✓	___	I practice self-discipline and self-control.
✓	___	I use my influence over others in a positive way.
✓	___	I have a positive attitude toward school.
✓	___	I know when I have contributed to a behavior problem or conflict.
✓	___	My friends are achievers and have positive attitudes about school.
✓	___	I try to have appropriate behavior.

Reproducible page for student use.

Academic Characteristics of Students Who Are Becoming Achievers…

Rate yourself in these areas. First, mark a check under **S** for all those items that indicate your strengths. Next, count the number of strengths you have checked. Then check **W** for weaknesses; BUT you are not allowed to check more weaknesses than strengths.

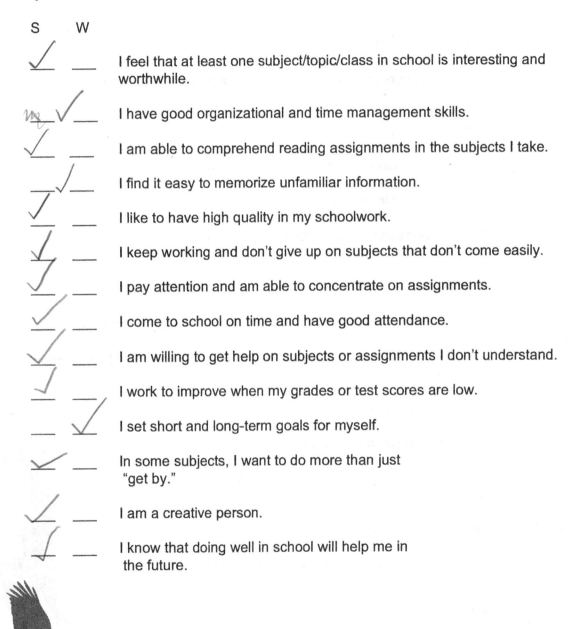

S   W

✓ ___ I feel that at least one subject/topic/class in school is interesting and worthwhile.

___ ✓ ___ I have good organizational and time management skills.

✓ ___ I am able to comprehend reading assignments in the subjects I take.

___ ✓ I find it easy to memorize unfamiliar information.

✓ ___ I like to have high quality in my schoolwork.

✓ ___ I keep working and don't give up on subjects that don't come easily.

✓ ___ I pay attention and am able to concentrate on assignments.

✓ ___ I come to school on time and have good attendance.

✓ ___ I am willing to get help on subjects or assignments I don't understand.

✓ ___ I work to improve when my grades or test scores are low.

___ ✓ I set short and long-term goals for myself.

✓ ___ In some subjects, I want to do more than just "get by."

✓ ___ I am a creative person.

✓ ___ I know that doing well in school will help me in the future.

Reproducible page for student use.

Your Peer Group – Your Friends

Your parents have probably asked you about your group of friends. From time to time, you may have felt they are too concerned about your peer group and your friendships. But their concern about peer pressure is genuine. In fact, if you have had any contact with your peers in the past month, you have probably faced some form of peer pressure.

What your friends think of you and the opinions other kids (who aren't necessarily your friends) have about you are essential in the development of your self-confidence. If someone put you down for wearing the wrong brand of clothes, having a strange hairstyle, doing something, or going somewhere that isn't "cool," or even speaking with an unfamiliar accent, you may have had your self-confidence weakened by your peers. When this happens, it's hard to keep feeling like an achiever! Think about Mario's story:

Fourteen-year-old Mario and his family have recently moved to a small southern town from a Boston suburb. He feels as if he is in a foreign country. Things are that different. Most of the kids in the ninth grade at his new school have known each other all their lives. They say "hi" to him but really don't include him in their activities. They talk so differently Mario has a hard time understanding them. But they say he has an accent! He hung out with his friends at the mall back home. But there's no mall in this town. No public transportation, either. Without a driver's license or friends, Mario's self-confidence is sinking quickly.

Kids like Mario who change schools or who move from one part of the country to another or from one country to another may lose confidence in themselves because of a new peer group.

Minority students, particularly African-Americans, often face a lot of peer pressure, which encourages them not to succeed in school. One mother, whose daughter is a highly intelligent black student who usually makes As, tells about her daughter's eighth grade report card:

"When she was in the eighth grade, there was a noticeable decline in her grades. When we talked about it, she told me she was the only black student in the gifted program at her school, and the other black students didn't like her. They said that because she got good grades, she was trying to 'act white.' She decided to make Cs instead. So she had sacrificed her grades for their friendship."

According to teachers, principals, and psychologists, many black students do this. They decide not to achieve because of peer pressure and because they fear they will be accused of "acting white." They also don't want to look smarter than their friends, and they want to be a part of the group. There have been many studies concerning this problem. In one study, a newspaper published in Columbia, South Carolina, reported that some black teenagers perform poorly in school to avoid criticism from their friends.

Black students are not alone in this situation. Any student who has friends who think getting good grades is "nerdy" or "uncool" has the same problem. It takes a lot of self-confidence to make your own decisions and set your own goals about what you want to do academically and then to work toward and achieve them.

Think About It!

Think about your friends and your relationship with them. Write how you think they feel about you as a friend. Then check it out.

Your best friend

nice, smart, funny, enthusiastic

Your other friends

helpful, nice, funny

Describe peer pressure you face at school. What do others want you to do or say?

How do you react to peer pressure?

I don't get easily offended because I know I'm better than that

Give an example of how peers boosted your self-confidence or wounded your self-confidence.

Helped   say Thank you to advice I give

Made Worse   laugh at me

What could you do about this?

try harder

Failure

It's written in big, bold letters so you wouldn't miss it. It's something we'd all like to avoid thinking about, but it's a fact of everyone's life. It may sound strange, but every successful person has been a failure at some point in his or her life. No one is a winner every time. For example, Michael Jordan failed to make his high school basketball team! There are kids (and adults, too) who never try to do anything because they are so afraid they might not do it right. They have a fear of failure.

A famous scientist and author Dr. Isaac Asimov once said, **_"Some things are worth a reasonable amount of hot water."_** In other words, you are not going to succeed and make everyone happy every time. You might get into "hot water" some of the time. You might make mistakes along the way. That's OK!

Any attempt to do something, even if it doesn't work out the way you'd hoped, is a victory…if you have the self-confidence to make the attempt. In fact, the worst failure in life is not to have tried at all.

Maybe you've thought of some things you'd like to try. Maybe you have some goals you think you can reach someday, but you are really hesitant to work on them. You may think you are not good enough or smart enough or talented enough to do them.

In the next chapter, you are going to think about setting some goals. Don't limit yourself and your attempts because you are afraid you might fail! If you do fail, **learn** from the experience and move on. That's what makes a successful person.

Think About It!

Now think about your fear of failure. What is one thing you would like to do that you have never done?

go on a trip/airplane by myself

What are you afraid will happen if you try it and don't succeed?

I will die

Then what would happen?

I would be dead

Then what would you do?

I wouldn't be able to do anything

What is the worst thing that could happen?

die

Using Failure as an Excuse

Some kids make excuses to and for themselves all the time. Have you heard anyone say things like this?

Why should I bother to study for that spelling test? I'm just going to fail it anyway.

I'm not doing the homework. I'm failing this class already, so I'm not wasting my time.

That teacher hates me. He'll fail me no matter what I do.

Why should I try to do anything my mom wants? She thinks everything I do is wrong no matter what.

All of those are examples of **negative self-talk**. People who talk to themselves in a negative way often use failure as an excuse for not attempting something in the first place. People who talk like this may sound tough and act as if they have everything under control, but on the inside, their self-confidence is very low.

Think about yourself. Did you ever use the **possibility** of failure as an excuse for not doing something at all? As you work on becoming an achiever, make sure you are not talking yourself into being a failure!

Think About It!

Someone once said, "The dictionary is not the only place where failure comes before success."
Is this saying true for your life? ___yes___

Why or why not?
because if you fail, it just makes you want to try that much harder

Fear of Success

Fear of success sounds like a contradiction in terms, doesn't it? But many kids are afraid of being successful. Some think that their friends won't like them as much, while others feel that once they are successful, their parents and teachers might expect quality work from them every time.

Being successful is a risk. But it's also an exciting adventure. If you are afraid of success, take the risk! Bart Conner, a gymnast who won two gold medals in the 1984 Summer Olympics, puts it this way: "Commit yourself and reach out a little farther than you necessarily think you can. Do something a little risky, and usually that will make you stand out above."

Think About It!

So, you have a fear of success? If so, what do you fear most?

that it will never happen

List risks you could take as you work to become an achiever.

- Try hard
- put effort into everything

How Does Success Happen?

You probably know an adult you consider to be a success. Perhaps this is a teacher, a coach, an aunt or uncle, a cousin, or a neighbor. It may surprise you to discover that this person, like almost every successful person, has had some obstacles to overcome along the road to success.

Use the following form as a guideline as you interview that person and reflect on what you can learn about your own life from his or her experiences.

Interviewing an Overcomer

A person who has overcome obstacles on the road to success

Name of person ___teacher_____

Obstacle(s) overcome _____

‑ study

‑ college

How it happened

‑study hard

‑went to college

How this could be a model for my life

I want to be a teacher, so I have to
study hard, get good grades + go
to college

My plan of action   study hard, get good grades,
go to college

© Pieces of Learning

2. Goal Setting

"Can't you just see me now?" Shaneka exclaimed to her best friend. "I'll be on the moon or maybe on Mars. There are all kinds of new things to discover. I'm going to look down at the earth and figure out a way to get rid of all our pollution. I'm going to be an astronaut... Just like Mae Jemison."

"I'm gonna find me some land and get out of the suburbs," declared Ryan. "I hate the traffic and all these houses that look alike. When I grow up, I hope I can wake up every morning, go outside, and work on my land. That's what my cousin does. Who knows? Maybe I'll grow Christmas trees!"

"We know how to speak both Spanish and English," Carlos and Felicia said to their teacher. "Our parents, well, they don't speak English much at all. We think lots of businesses are going to need people that can speak both languages."

Their teacher nodded. "I bet there will be lots of work throughout the 21st Century for people who can do what you two can do."

Your Dreams for the Future

Like the students above, all of you have hopes and dreams for the future. Some of your dreams will change a thousand times before you're an adult, and some will probably stay pretty much the same. Either way, all of your hopes and dreams are important. They are the building blocks of motivation and can help you in setting your goals, giving you purpose, and deciding on your direction in life.

Most of us have many different dreams. Some of our dreams are very practical while others are just what we've labeled them – **dreams**. As you go through school and as you get older, you'll start deciding which ones are realistic to pursue. Dreams don't magically come true. They usually gradually become reality through your experiences, through the encouragement of others, through hard work, and through the examples of people you know personally, have read about, or have seen on television.

**HOPES AND DREAMS
ARE BUILDING BLOCKS OF MOTIVATION**

Maybe you've already experienced "dream motivation." If your dad was on the swim team when he was a boy, he may have already inspired you to sign up for swimming lessons. If your family is musical, they may have encouraged you to play in the band. If a veterinarian came to talk at your school, you may have decided you'd like to work with animals. Whatever your dreams, they are easier to accomplish when you have some adult to help you, encourage you, and give you advice when you need it.

A GOAL IS A DREAM WITH A DEADLINE. – HARVEY MACKAY

Goals and dreams work hand in hand.
You have to have the dream
in order to know what goals you want to pursue.
And you have to have a plan
to accomplish the goals.
Working on the plan and your goals
can turn your dream into reality!

Think About It!

What are your hopes and dreams? Write three of them.

* go to college

* pro. tennis player

* teacher

Now write the names of three people who have inspired you to pursue these hopes and dreams or people you could talk to about making your hopes and dreams a reality.

1. my techers

2. my parents

3. Ms. Sherri

As one of your short-term goals plan to see or talk to at least one of the people listed above within the next 10 days. Discuss your hopes and dreams with them. Begin a journal of ideas they have given you.

At the beginning of his career, football coach Lou Holtz made a list of 107 things he wanted to do before he died. This list covered all kinds of interesting things, including eating dinner at the White House and learning to sky dive. Coach Holtz believed that success comes when you **write down your goals** and then decide exactly what to do in order to achieve them. By the time he retired, he had achieved most of his goals! You, too, can be an achiever as you learn to turn your goals into reality.

Holtz often asked three questions he thought would determine whether a person would be a success or a failure. How would you answer them?

1. Can people trust me to do my best?
2. Am I committed to the task at hand?
3. Do I care about other people and show it?

If the answers to all three questions are yes, there is no way you can fail. – Lou Holtz

Turning Your Dreams into Reality

In the last few pages, you've been dreaming a little as you've been thinking about your future. Now ask yourself, *"Can I really achieve these hopes and dreams? Can I turn the dreams into goals and the goals into reality?"* If you hope to be an Olympic swimmer, but you don't know how to swim, and never plan to learn, that goal will never be an achievable one! If you want to be a mechanical engineer, but you're much better in language arts than you are in math, you may want to reconsider.

No matter what your hopes and dreams are, there are three more important questions to ask yourself:

1. What is really important to me?
2. Am I ready to spend my time and energy doing the things I need to do – the things to help myself change my hopes and dreams into goals? Am I ready to proceed to achieve them?
3. Will I be able to keep on working toward these goals and not get discouraged in times of small defeats?

If you can answer the first question and answer **YES** to the other two, you have taken the first big step in turning your dreams into goals and your goals into reality. If you can't answer yes, where might you end up? Write down your thoughts.

Work = achievement of goal   No work = <u>no achievement of goal</u>

**GOALS ARE DIFFERENT FROM HOPES AND DREAMS
BECAUSE WITH GOALS YOU NEED <u>TO ACT</u>
IN ORDER TO ACHIEVE THEM**

Dreams are more pleasant than goals, because dreams don't take any work or energy. But goals do take hard work, sometimes over a long period of time.

Life is Like a Football Game

Think about how a football game is played. How are touchdowns made?

At the kick-off, does the receiver catch the ball and run all the way down the field for a touchdown? Possibly. It **could** happen, but it doesn't happen that way very often. Usually the receiver begins running with the ball and someone tackles him. Then, through a series of well-planned plays, the team usually advances ten yards and gets a first down. In football, you don't gain yardage on every play. Sometimes you get pushed back, and you have to try harder and sometimes try a different approach to make up the lost ground.

Scoring a touchdown and then winning a game or the championship is a long process that takes a lot of planning and a lot of work. Life is like that, too. It is **possible** to become an "over-night success" and become rich and famous, just like it is **possible** to make a touchdown on the first kickoff. But it **probably** won't happen. Becoming an achiever in school, and later on becoming a successful adult, takes lots of planning and lots of work. In the game called "life" there will be many times when you'll get knocked down or pushed back. There may be times when you think everyone is "playing" better than you are or has been given a better position.

The problem is that many young people get discouraged when something goes wrong. Many kids don't want to do all the planning and all the work involved in becoming an achiever. Suppose that happened at a football game. Suppose a player said, *"I got tackled and lost yardage. I give up. I quit."* That sounds crazy, doesn't it? But kids do it every day when it comes to their schoolwork and their future. They just give up. And what happens? They sit on the bench all through their lives.

Think About It!

Why is it not a good idea to "sit on the bench" in your schoolwork and in your future?

because you won't get anything done, you are just resting the whole time

Kids who are becoming achievers don't give up. They are willing to work hard and learn from their mistakes and setbacks. They have a game plan, just like the football coach does. And they know where they want to go because they have goals.

When you play football, you know the direction you're going and why you are heading there. You know where the yard lines are, where the goal posts are, and you keep heading in the right direction. This is what goal setting does for your life.

In some ways, life is very much like a football game, but in other ways it is not. Consider a kick-off — the first day of school. A touchdown might be an "A." Think about a penalty, half time, 1st down, 4th down, interception, incomplete pass, completed pass, time out, coach, team, spectator, and a cheerleader.

Think About It!!

Compare your life to a football game in 3 ways.

1. achieving a goal is like winning a game
2. running past all the people are the obsticales
3. training for a game is like studying

Now write down 3 ways that it is not like a football game at all.

1. there aren't "different quarters" in life
2. you don't have someone (a coach) guiding you your whole life
3. ?

A final word about life and football games! Most football teams have fans who cheer them on when they win and when they lose. Who cheers you on? Write their names below.

Mom, dad, friends, family

For what reason do you want them to continue cheering you on?

It makes you want to keep working

They are your greatest assets in becoming an achiever! Tell them!

Goals in Many Sports and Games

Most sports and games have specific goals. Achieving the goal usually results in getting some points. The points add up to the final score. In many games, there are smaller goals along the way. For example, in baseball a small goal would be to make a hit and get to first base, but what you really want to do is get home and score a run.

Look at the goals in the list of sports and games below. Can you add more?

The golf "goal" = cup or hole
The football "goal" = goal posts
The soccer "goal" = net
The basketball "goal" = hoop

Baseball = home run
Monopoly = ~~4~~ houses
Trivial Pursuit = ?
Uno = least/no cards

Your ideas _____   _____

_____   _____

Think About It!

Why do some goals have boundaries?

because if there weren't boundaries, you wouldn't need to work to achieve your goal

_____

Should your goals have limits? Why or why not?

no. you should be able to achieve whatever you want to

What Can You Learn from the World of Sports?

Below are 15 sports ideas to encourage top performance. They are also very useful concepts for other parts of life. Write your ideas about how these could apply to your life in school or at home. Discuss with a friend, your parents, or another adult.

1. Show up both for practice and for the main event.

   Show up for practice + tournament

2. Practice skills before the big performance.

   study for a test

3. Know where you're heading and know what the goal is.

   college — pro. tennis

4. Have several game plans, not just one.

   if something goes wrong with plan A, move to plan B

5. Don't count on the one thing that is the least likely to occur.

   work hard for it

6. Work toward small goals (short-term goals) to reach larger goals.

   good idea

7. Don't give up because you get a penalty or make a mistake.

   keep working until you get it right

8. Figure out what you want to accomplish and then plan backwards.

   ✓

9. Have a coach and have people who cheer you on.

   makes you want to work even harder

10. Know the rules and abide by them.

    2

11. Have the right equipment and know how to use it.

    will get you far

12. Listen to the referee.

    so you don't make the same mistake again

13. Work as a team to get things done.

    ✓

14. Strive to beat your personal best.

    ✓

15. You don't need to win every time to be a big success.

    you can try harder the next time

The Story of Philip

From the time he was 10 years old, Philip wanted to go to college at the same school his mom and dad had attended. They told him it was "very selective," but he wasn't sure what that meant. Still, the goal was in his head, and he knew he needed to work toward it. When he was in sixth grade, he decided to write to the college and ask for information about admission requirements. He found out that to be considered for admission, he needed to get all A's and B's in high school and get a high score on the SAT.

Philip started planning backwards. In order to get A's and B's in high school, he needed to have a good academic background in middle school. He learned he needed to study, and he began reading and increasing his vocabulary for the SAT. Philip had six years to plan backwards for his goal. He had to work hard every grading period and even went to summer school for additional help in math. Most of his friends didn't have a game plan for their lives, but Philip did.

When Philip began his senior year of high school, he was ready with his college application. He had the qualifications and thought he would achieve his goal of getting into the college of his choice. His friends were surprised to learn how difficult it was to get into a "good" school. They had goals, but they hadn't planned backwards.

The college Philip chose accepted him. His friends said, "Oh, Philip's a brain, and he's just lucky." Philip felt they were wrong. He believed he had accomplished his goal through planning backwards and then doing a lot of hard work. What do you think?

Planning Backwards

One way to plan your strategy for accomplishing your goals is to plan backwards. That is, start with the final goal and then plan backwards to see how you might get there.

In becoming an achiever, set some short-term and long-term goals for yourself. On the next page, you will find a form that will help you. If you want to try planning backwards, begin with the section that says "After high school" and then work backwards to the top of the page. If you have trouble thinking of goals, use the forms on pages 33, 34, and 35 along with a parent, friend, or teacher to help you in your decision making.

Remember, we don't always accomplish every goal we attempt! Even when you plan backwards, what you are working toward doesn't always happen. That is why it is good to have more than one goal and more than one game plan for your life. For this reason the forms on the next few pages all ask for more than one goal.

GOAL SETTING

WHERE DO YOU WANT TO GO – HOW DO YOU PLAN TO GET THERE?

1. What school-related goals will you work toward during the next grading period?

a. good grades

b. A's on Test

c. principal's honor roll

How will you achieve these goals?

study/listen in class
study
good grades

During this school year?

a. good grades

b. principal's honor roll

study/listen in class
good grades

After high school?

a. go to college

b. pass college

work hard
achieve goals

2. What personal goals would you like to achieve in the next 6 months?

a. get to the top 10 in GA

b. get good grades in school

c. _____

How will you achieve these goals?

work hard @ practice + play lots of tournaments
study

Within the next year or two?

a. same as above

b. _____

Reproducible page for student use.

PROBLEM SOLVING, GOAL SETTING & DECISION MAKING

Step 1: List some of your hopes and dreams.

PRo tennis player

Step 2: With at least one other person, brainstorm possible goals that you could achieve from your hopes and dreams. When brainstorming, all ideas are accepted!

GOALS

-get good grades in school
-practice hard at practice

Step 3: In the space below, list positive points and negative points about the goals you listed.

<u>Pos.</u>

- will achieve my goal

<u>Neg</u>

- study(may take a long time)

Step 4: In the space below, list one or more goals you will work toward. Begin planning backwards with the time line.

GOAL   **TIME LINE**

PRo· tennis player

pass college

© Pieces of Learning

MINDMAP - PROBLEM SOLVING, GOAL SETTING & DECISION MAKING

Complete the circles with your goal and steps to achieve it. Then number the circles in the order you need to attack your goal.

② practice hard

① get good grades

pro tennis player
Goal

⑤ learn mental game

③ pass college

④ learn physical game

Reproducible page for student use.

Again think of your life as a series of football games. For each game, you need to have a goal to aim for, like the goal line in the game. This is called a **long-term goal**, and it may take some time to accomplish it. You also need a way to get down the field through the 50, 40, 30, 20, and 10-yard lines. These are your **short-term goals**. They don't take as long to achieve, but each one of them puts you nearer your final goal. You might want to think about it like this:

My Game Plan

My long-term goal is ...to be on the honor roll in math.

Short-term Goal — Do my math homework every night.

50 — — — — — — — — — — — — — — — — — —

Short-term Goal — Study facts, definitions, and problems before each test.

40 — — — — — — — — — — — — — — — — — —

Short-term Goal — See the teacher whenever I don't understand something.

30 — — — — — — — — — — — — — — — — — —

Short-term Goal — Review any test problems I get wrong so that I understand them next time.

20 — — — — — — — — — — — — — — — — — —

Short-term Goal — Study with a friend who understands math well.

10 — — — — — — — — — — — — — — — — — —

Touchdown!
Goal Achieved! Math Grade B+

My Game Plan

My Long-Term Goal is to _be a pro tennis player_

Short-Term Goal
50 — — — — — — — — — — —
study hard

Short-Term Goal
40 — — — — — — — — — —
get good grades

Short-Term Goal
30 — — — — — — — — — —
practice hard @ practice

Short-Term Goal
20 — — — — — — — — —
stay fit

Short-Term Goal
10 — — — — — — — — —
try hard even if you fail

Possible penalties _forget about a big test,_
miss a night of practice

Touchdown!   Goal Achieved!

Reproducible page for student use.

3. Motivation

Meet Leo

Leo is having lots of problems at home. His parents went through a divorce two years ago, and his dad often fails to send the child support check. It seems to Leo that his mother is always unhappy. She has a job, but it isn't enough to make ends meet. Leo is in 7th grade and finds school hard. His teachers think he is a behavior problem. He knows he should study, but he really doesn't feel like it in school, and he doesn't feel like it when he gets home from school. He used to think he was smart enough to get a college scholarship someday, but he just doesn't care about that anymore.

You probably know lots of kids like Leo. In fact, he might be a lot like you. Leo thinks life has been pretty unfair to him. He sees other kids at school with nice clothes and happy families, and that really makes him depressed and angry. He admits that he isn't putting forth much effort in school as far as his studies are concerned. In fact, he puts most of his effort into thinking of ways he can annoy the teacher. It's no wonder they call him a behavior problem!

One of Leo's basic problems is that he has lost his **motivation** for achievement. He says he doesn't feel like studying in school, and he doesn't feel like studying at home either…BUT…I wonder . . . how many kids really do feel like studying? After all, it's hard work! Nevertheless, some kids decide that the work is worth it. Their motivation comes from inside. They have decided which things are worth their efforts.

Everyone is motivated to do something! Leo is motivated to give his teachers a hard time by being a behavior problem. Achievers are motivated to study and learn, even when the work is hard, and even when they don't feel like it.

Think About It!

What things are you motivated to do?

- go to school
- play tennis

Motivation: What is it and How Does it Work?

Motivation is the drive and desire for success in whatever you are doing. It requires dedication in terms of focusing on and working toward a goal. Positive motivation also involves having a sense of purpose, a feeling of enthusiasm for what you are doing and for what you are working toward, and an ability to make good choices and move yourself in the right direction.

Motivation comes from two main sources – from within yourself (**internal motivation**) or from an outside influence (**external motivation**). When you're motivated to do something, it's often a combination of the two. For example, you might be motivated to design a nice cover for your history report because you enjoy drawing. You know you will do a good job, you know you will enjoy doing it, and you know that you'll be proud of the finished product. **That's internal motivation**.

However, you also know the teacher will give you 25 extra credit points if you turn in the report with a good cover design, and you can use the 25 points. The 25 points from the teacher is **external motivation**. The fact that you're motivated to design the cover is a combination of internal and external motivation.

People are usually motivated **internally** to do things that interest them. Almost everyone has a special interest. Sometimes adults say, *"The only thing kids are interested in is sitting around and watching TV or playing on the computer."* I disagree! It is true that most kids like TV and computers, but in talking with groups of students, I've found that kids today have a wide range of other interests. Here are some examples. You can see how many different interests there are!

- Learning how to help the homeless

- Designing swords and shields from the Middle Ages

- Building houses with Habitat for Humanity

- Playing a musical instrument

- Making Models

- Karate and martial arts

- Civil War re-enactments

- Rockets and space science

- Scuba Diving

- Ballet Dancing

Think About It!

What are your areas of special interest?

tennis

Write three topics/areas of special interest to you.

—_tennis_

—_T.V._

—_shopping_

Are any of these interests related to things that motivate you on page 38?
If so, which ones?

yes — tennis

Do these areas of special interest relate to the goals you have set for
yourself? In what way?

yes — to become a pro.

Remember, it will probably be easier to motivate yourself internally when
you are working on areas that interest you.

On the other hand, did you have trouble listing topics or areas of interest?
If so, the suggestions on the next page will help you.

**MOTIVATION
IS PUTTING WORK CLOTHES
ON YOUR DREAM**

NO SPECIAL INTEREST? – SOME SUGGESTIONS

Sometimes it's difficult for kids to know what interests them. If you really don't know your interests, here are some suggestions to help you discover them.

Check the ones you might want to try.   **I tried this on this date**

__Go to your local library and plan to spend at least a couple of hours   _____
there. Skim through magazines, reference books, newspapers, almanacs,
and any other information sources the library has. Write down all of the
topics of possible interest to you. Before you leave, check out at least one
book to broaden your knowledge of a topic.

__Watch a TV, video, or DVD about a subject you don't know very much   _____
about. See what you can learn. Discuss with a parent or other adult.

__Find out about places in your community that need volunteer workers.   _____
Volunteer your time. Places of worship, nursing homes, and non-profit
agencies are good places to look.

__Try building, drawing, or creating something with your hands.   _____

__Visit museums and take the time to read the exhibits and learn about   _____
the displays.

__If you belong to Scouts, work on merit badges. These give you the   _____
opportunity to explore many areas of interest.

__Visit a local newspaper office and see how they get news from around   _____
the world.

__Use an Internet search engine to find topics of interest. Then investigate   _____
how you could learn more about a specific topic.

Get suggestions from others about their special interests and hobbies: _____

Classmates _____

Teachers _____

Family members _____

Friends _____

Use the Resident Expert Planning Form on the next page to record what you learn once you find a topic of special interest.

RESIDENT EXPERT PLANNING FORM

Topic: tennis

Things I already know about this topic: (Use other side of paper if needed)

- how to play

What I want to learn about this topic:

- more technique

Resources I could use:

- coach
- book
- computer

My learning plan with checkpoint dates:

	Activity	Checkpoint date
1.	go to practice	
2.	read a tennis magazine	
3.		
4.		

Learning Styles and Modalities

How we learn affects our motivation. **Learning style or learning modality is the term for how each person learns**. People are usually motivated to learn those things that match well with their styles or modalities. There are many tests that help you discover your own learning style. You may have taken some of these in school. On the next 3 pages you will find checklists you can use to determine both your learning style and learning modality. Complete them and then finish the remainder of this page.

Think About It!

Which learning styles and modalities best describe you?

flash cards, quizzing me on the material

What types of activities are you most motivated to do based on your learning style and modality?

make flashcards for all vocab. words

Sample Activities and Products

audio tapes/CDs
books
brainstorming
charts and diagrams
debates
experiments
games
group work
hands-on activities
independent study

learning centers
lecture
movies
oral reports
PowerPoint presentations
projects
skits
television
workbooks
Webquests

LEARNING STYLES CHECKLIST

Check items in each category that describe you. The strongest learning style or styles will be those with the most items checked.

Concrete sequential students like to:

_____ Read or listen to, and then follow directions.

___✓___ Take notes, look at charts or diagrams, and make outlines.

___✓___ Participate in structured learning, including pencil and paper exercises.

___✓___ Have an organized teacher.

___✓___ Know what the grading system is and the teacher's specific expectations.

Abstract sequential students like to:

_____ Read different kinds of books, usually sequentially from beginning to end.

___✓___ Listen to audio tapes, CDs, and lectures; see videos, films and slides; work on the computer and other electronic learning tools.

___✓___ Help other students understand the subject matter or what they've read.

___✓___ Find THE answer to a problem, and are uncomfortable with multiple answers and possibilities.

_____ Look at things logically, even situations where a logical solution is not necessarily the best one nor does it solve the problem.

Concrete random students like to:

___✓___ Complete a product or project for a classroom assignment.

___✓___ Brainstorm creative ideas.

_____ Take risks. Concrete random students will volunteer for anything!

_____ Do things by trial and error.

___✓___ Solve problems alone.

_____ Avoid IQ and achievement tests.

Abstract random students like to:

_____ Listen to, learn from, and respond to their classmates.

___✓___ Work in groups and will become the natural leaders in small groups.

_____ Do short reading assignments and often do not read books sequentially.

_____ Use emotions and intuition.

___✓___ Have lots of things going on at once.

Reproducible for student use.

LEARNING MODALITIES CHECKLIST

Check items in each category that describe you. The strongest learning modality or modalities will be those with the most items checked.

Visual learners
- ☐ Are good with detail
- ☑ Learn by seeing, watching demonstrations
- ☑ Often remember whatever they have written down
- ☑ Can recall the placement of words and pictures on a page
- ☑ Like descriptive reading
- ☑ Enjoy and learn from visual displays and colors
- ☑ Recognize words by sight and people by face rather than name
- ☑ Have a vivid imagination and think in pictures
- ☐ Are deliberate problem solvers and plan solutions in advance
- ☑ Facial expressions are a good indication of their emotions

Auditory/Verbal learners
- ☑ Enjoy listening but are always ready to talk
- ☑ Like music, rap, poetry, rhyming words
- ☑ Enjoy dialogues, skits, and debates
- ☐ Have auditory word attack skills and learn words phonetically
- ☐ Talk to themselves, repeating information aloud
- ☑ Are distracted by sounds
- ☐ Talk out problems and the pros and cons of a situation
- ☑ Express emotion through changes in pitch, tone, and volume of voice
- ☐ Are not detail persons; tend to be global thinkers
- ☑ Learn through verbal instructions from others or themselves

Reproducible for student use.

⇒

Motivation

Kinesthetic/Tactile learners

☑ Learn by hands-on experiences

☑ Prefer direct involvement rather than being a spectator

☑ Enjoy the performing arts and/or athletics

☑ Like working with materials, machinery, and tools

☑ Prefer action/adventure stories and DVD's

☐ Communicate feelings through body language

☐ Experiment with ideas to see how they will work in the real world

☑ Touch, feel, manipulate, and play with objects

☑ Show emotions physically by jumping, hugging, applauding, etc.

☐ Remember what they have done rather than what they have seen or read

Technological learners

☐ Are mechanically oriented

☐ Know how to use technological tools without formal instruction

☐ Enjoy using a video camera

☐ Obtain much of their information electronically

☐ Like integrated learning activities

☐ Would like to learn everything via the computer

☐ Spend much of their spare time on the computer or playing video games

☐ Know how to work with and use new software and hardware

☐ Interact and communicate with others via the Internet

☐ Understand how to integrate various technologies

Reproducible for student use.

Meet Kathy

Kathy and her mom live alone. Kathy's father was killed in a car accident when she was a baby, so it seems she has always had just one parent. Her mom works as a nurse's aide at the hospital and goes to school two nights a week. Kathy is in 8th grade and studies hard. They don't have much money, but Kathy's goal is to go to college when she graduates from high school, and she hopes to get a full scholarship.

Sometimes schoolwork is really boring, and Kathy doesn't feel like studying. When that happens, she times herself. For every half hour she studies, she rewards herself with 10 minutes of listening to her favorite music or 10 minutes of talking on the phone to her best friend. Kathy's hard work is paying off. She is an achiever.

External Motivators – Invent Your Own

It's easy to feel motivated to do something when it interests you. However, sometimes we have to find the motivation to do things that aren't much fun, things that are boring, things that we're not interested in, and things that seem senseless. This usually requires **external motivation**. Teachers and parents often motivate kids in this way. For example, parents may tell their children tthey will receive some money or a special treat if they get good grades or successfully complete a project. Teachers may use things like computer time, stickers, prizes, or special privileges as external motivators for their students.

In becoming an achiever, you need to learn to create your own external motivators instead of waiting for your parents or teachers to do it. Achievers take on the responsibility of accomplishing goals and tasks, even doing those things they don't really feel like doing. The next time you really don't feel like doing something, but you know you need to do it, invent your own external motivators, and reward yourself for getting the task done.

Think About It!

What are some ways you could motivate yourself?

Things I Need to Do	How I can reward and motivate myself
–get good grades	–think about how I can become a pro. tennis player with good grades

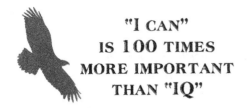

"I CAN"
IS 100 TIMES
MORE IMPORTANT
THAN "IQ"

Ability or Effort?

There's a lot of truth in that statement! Many students think that the kids who get good grades are just naturally smart and that they really don't have to study very much at all. However, the facts show quite a different story. Most achievers have **learned** to study and put a lot of effort into their schoolwork.

In Japan, the teachers think very little about their students' IQ's. They believe that everyone has the ability to succeed in school if they put forth the effort, and, in general, that is what Japanese students do. It is the same for us. If you have lacked motivation because you think you really aren't very smart anyway, think again! When you put forth the effort to learn and study something, over time it will begin to make sense to you. Eventually your test scores will go up and your grades will improve. You might even begin to enjoy the subject. Effort – hard work — will pay off in the end.

Think About It!

Which subjects are ones in which I have high ability? What motivates me to do well in those subjects?

Math. Nothing, it just comes natrully

Into which subjects do I have to put the most effort? What can I use to motivate me to do better?

Social studies. My friends or family or teacher(s)

What do I do with this information? Considering what I've written above, my plan for next week is:

I'm out of school, so I don't have a school related plan for next week

People Helping People

Roberto hung around with the "wrong crowd" for a long time. Most of the kids in the crowd were high school dropouts who didn't have jobs or didn't think much about the future. Roberto dropped out of high school in 11th grade, but he had a job stocking shelves at a local supermarket. This was where he met José. José, a senior in high school, began talking to Roberto about going back to school. Soon Roberto started thinking seriously about it, and José's constant encouragement motivated him to return to school. Today Roberto is a high school graduate and attends community college.

Joanetta, a fifth grader, adores her Aunt Lucy. Aunt Lucy is only 35 years old, and already she is a partner in a law firm. She is the only black and the only female in the firm, and Joanetta knows she is tops. Joanetta sets high goals for herself because she wants to follow in her aunt's footsteps. Aunt Lucy is her inspiration and motivation.

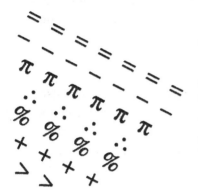

At the beginning of the school year, Tiffany didn't like math at all. She had never done well in math, and she was not interested in it. Heather was new to the school, and she and Tiffany became good friends. Heather wasn't good in math either, but the two girls made an important decision. They decided to become "study buddies" in math and help each other learn. A funny thing happened. The two girls became the two best math students in the class. They had motivated each other to study and understand math.

How Other People Can Help Your Motivation

Being motivated is not something you must do all by yourself. While it is important for you to take responsibility for your own motivation, most achievers have help from others to sustain their motivation over the long term. The most obvious people to help you are your teachers, parents, and friends, but there are other people who can assist you as well. As you can see in the stories of Roberto, Joanetta, Tiffany, and Heather, the people you work with, a special relative, or a friend who studies with you can be sources of motivation.

People who are special sources of motivation tend to fall into several categories. They may be **mentors** or **role models** or **study partners** or **peer tutors**.

Mentors – Mentors are people who have already succeeded at something you might like to do and are willing to give you advice, guidance, and motivation as you do it. A mentor can be a relative, friend, acquaintance, or an assigned mentor. The most important thing about a mentor is that he or she takes an interest in you and is willing to help you over an extended period of time.

Some schools have mentorship programs that match students with mentors. In other schools, mentorship develops without the help of a formal program. A mentor helps you stay motivated by encouraging and advising you. Occasionally, a mentor will not work well with a student. If this happens to you, do not be discouraged! Instead, find another mentor.

Role Models – A role model is a person you can look up to and hope to be like. In some ways, role models are similar to mentors, but you may not know your role model personally. Many times, sports stars, movie stars, or other famous people serve as role models. But a role model may also be a teacher, a neighbor, or a relative like Joanetta's Aunt Lucy. A role model can motivate you to do your best, achieve at your highest level, and work hard.

One problem with role models is that they may turn out to be quite different from your ideal of who they are. Some famous people who have been role models for kids have had personal problems such as an addiction to drugs or alcohol. It is important to remember that following the good example of a role model is an excellent motivation, but don't lose the motivation if your role model's behavior ends up disappointing you!

Study Partners – It's amazing how much you can learn by studying with someone else. A good study partner is usually a friend who has just about the same ability as you have in a given subject. When two people decide to study together and make a commitment to do so, each one motivates the other. For example, if one person really doesn't feel like studying on a particular evening, his or her partner can give the encouragement needed to study anyway. With a study partner, you tend to be more motivated because you don't want to disappoint the other person. In addition, studying can be more interesting and more enjoyable when it's done with someone else. Heather and Tiffany are good examples of study partners who have helped one another.

Study partners must decide how often they will study together and how long each study session will be. During that time, they must make sure they really do study. If you have a study partner who wants to laugh, talk, and fool around instead of studying, this will not work. In fact, you will find yourself studying less than if you studied alone. But if you can find a good study partner, someone who also wants to be an achiever, this can be an enjoyable way to become a more successful student.

Peer Tutors – A peer tutor is more advanced than you are in a given subject but is close to your age. A peer tutor will help you as you study, explaining concepts and ideas that you may not understand. Peer tutors are somewhat like teachers, but there is a big difference. They are students, just like you are, and often they can explain things in different ways so that you can understand them better than the way the teacher explains them.

A peer tutor may be in your class at school or may be a grade or two ahead of you. Some schools have peer tutor programs, but if yours doesn't, you can find a peer tutor easily. Ask the smartest person in your class if he or she will study with you and explain some of the work that you don't understand. Usually this person will be glad to help. Ask your teacher to give you the names of two or three kids in the next higher grade (for example, 8th graders if you're a 7th grader) who could help you. Some kids are embarrassed to ask for help, but most who are willing to ask find that working with a peer tutor gives them a much better understanding of subjects with which they were having trouble. Peer tutors often will motivate you to study more in depth and may give you the knowledge you need to become an achiever!

I HEAR AND I FORGET.
I SEE AND I REMEMBER.
I DO AND I UNDERSTAND.

CONFUCIUS

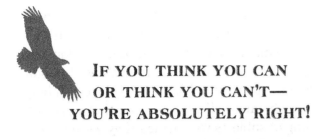

Success and Failure: How They Affect Motivation

IF YOU THINK YOU CAN OR THINK YOU CAN'T— YOU'RE ABSOLUTELY RIGHT!

Believe that you can succeed and expect success! That's an important key to being motivated.

Success is like having poison ivy, except that it feels better! But like poison ivy, it spreads. Have you ever noticed that when you've been successful at doing something, you feel good about everything else, too? Maybe you are a good soccer player. When your team wins the game and you've played well, you feel really happy. Not just about the soccer game, but about everything in general. That's how success works.

Like success, failure can breed more failure, but this doesn't have to happen. Everyone, even the smartest, most successful people, has experienced failure. What happens next depends on how a person deals with the failure. If a person looks at failures and mistakes as chances to grow and learn, he or she is actually benefiting from them. Some of the most successful people say, *"I won't make that mistake again!"* or *"I don't make the same mistake twice!"* What they're really saying is that they're learning from their failures.

Below are quotes about success and failure. Read them and then think of one of your own.

"FAILURE IS THE OPPORTUNITY TO BEGIN AGAIN MORE INTELLIGENTLY." –THOMAS JEFFERSON

"I ENJOY THE PROCESS (OF WORKING) AND DON'T WORRY ABOUT FAILING." –BALLERINA JANIE PARKER

"YOU CAN'T SUCCEED WITHOUT FAILURE. YOU HAVE TO HAVE LOTS OF FAILURES ON THE ROAD TO SUCCESS." – ARTIST ROBERT KIPNISS

Your thoughts on success and failure:

both success + failure make you want to keep striving for your goal but success boosts your confidence + failure doesn't

There are some people who say, *"I'm just a failure. I'll never amount to anything,"*

Maybe you've felt that way when you've made a mistake or failed at something you had hoped to do well. Students, who feel like failures and decide they are not smart enough to please the teachers or do the assignments correctly, often decide to stop trying. Their motivation to learn ceases to exist, and they waste weeks, months, and years just sitting in school feeling like failures, and doing nothing.

Think About It!

Think about some times you have felt successful. These don't have to be related to schoolwork. Remember how good you felt about the event and about yourself. Write about one of those times. Then share the situation with a partner or small group.

When I finally got an A on my
science test, it made me feel
really good about myself and I knew
all the hard work paid off

This is the mindset you want to have as you approach your work in school. Just as a coach psychs up the team before a game, you have to psych up yourself – motivate yourself – to be a successful student.

4. Time Management and Organization

Finding something in Emily's locker is a major miracle. In fact, when she opens her locker, things fall out all over the hall, and she has to stuff them back in to close it! Her room at home looks the same. It is almost impossible to walk across the floor because of all the junk that is piled there. Emily's mom closes the door to her room and tells Emily, "It's your problem." Emily is a good student but loses so many of her completed assignments that she ends up getting C's instead of A's and B's.

Ali is in trouble with everyone. He forgets his homework assignments, he forgets where he put his glasses, he forgets which books he should take to school, and he even forgot his mother's birthday! His friends tease him and call him the "absent-minded professor," but his lack of organization is becoming a real problem.

Nikki does well on the homework that is assigned one day and is due the next, but she is not so good at completing long-range projects and reports. She thinks she has plenty of time to do them, so she doesn't worry about them, and suddenly they're due the next day.

Becoming Organized

Emily, Ali, and Nikki all have problems with organization. Emily's "stuff" is not organized. The number of things Emily has in her locker and in her room has become a barrier to her becoming an achiever. Ali does not take time to "think clearly." He doesn't remember to do the everyday tasks that would help him to become more organized. And while Nikki is organized for the short term, she has not thought about doing long-range planning.

Maybe you are disorganized like Emily, Ali, or Nikki. If you are developing self-confidence, are setting your goals, and feel motivated, the next step in your action plan is to get organized. Being organized is one of the most important skills to learn in becoming an achiever. Some people seem to be "naturally organized" without putting forth any effort, but most of us are "all over the page;" we don't "have our ducks in a row" and have to work at developing organizational skills!

On the next page you can test yourself to see how organized you are.

IN THE LONG RUN
WE ONLY HIT
WHAT WE AIM AT

HENRY DAVID THOREAU

Organization Quiz

Mark a check under **Yes** or **No** to indicate how organized you are.

No   Yes

___ ✓   1. There are things in my locker or backpack that I haven't looked at in a month or more.

___ ✓   2. At home, I have a pile of newspapers, comic books, or magazines that I haven't read yet but that I'm going to read some day.

✓ ___   3. I never write down assignments because I think I can remember everything that is important.

✓ ___   4. I forget about long-range assignments until it's too late to do a good job on them.

___ ✓   5. My parents keep track of my schedule of after-school activities, and I just do whatever they tell me I'm scheduled to do.

___ ✓   6. I leave at least one of the following: lunch money, notebooks, homework, notes that are supposed to be signed, etc. at home on the average of once a week.   *middle*

___ ✓   7. I have a hard time keeping track of my keys, glasses, purse, wallet, or other necessary items.

✓ ___   8. I have trouble remembering important dates like anniversaries, birthdays, class field trips, test dates, etc.

___ ✓   9. When I start on an assignment or project, I have a hard time completing it because I get distracted easily.

✓ ___   10. I keep telling myself, "I've got to get organized," but I never do.

3   7   TOTALS

SCORING

10, 9 OR 8	Yes – You have major problems with organization!
7 or 6	Yes – You need to develop additional organizational skills.
5, 4 or 3	Yes – You have good organizational skills but can still improve.
2, 1, or 0	Yes – You have excellent organizational skills!

The test helps to pinpoint areas where you need assistance in becoming more organized. If you look at the items where you marked "Yes," you will see which areas are organizational problems for you. Nearly everyone needs to become more organized and to develop better organizational skills in some areas. The next few pages of this chapter will help you do that.

Reproducible page for student use.

Organization Quiz

What Your Answers Mean

Now that you have taken the Organization Quiz and identified your weak areas (the items you answered "yes"), read about each item to find out more about your specific organization problems.

Number 1:

This is the "pack rat" question. If you answered yes to this question, you probably keep too much of your "stuff" and are not good at distinguishing which items are important and which are not. Make sure you clean out your backpack, desk, etc. every week. Sort the items into piles such as *Throw Away Now, Use This Week, Put Away in the Correct Place, Do Something With This Today,* etc. Have the trash can handy and don't be afraid to use it!

Number 2:

This is a planning question. The worst thing about the word "someday" is that it never comes! Decide the date and time you are going to do the thing you say you will do "someday." If you can't decide on when, the piles of things you've been saving for "someday" need to go!

Number 3:

You probably don't write down assignments for one reason — you don't want to do them! Not writing them down becomes the convenient excuse! You might want to try to write them down on Post-it® Notes. You can stick the note directly on the book or paper itself. Generally, 80% of things you write down you will actually accomplish. So writing assignments on a Post-it® Note is a good first step.

Number 4:

Forgetting about long-range assignments is a major problem for most disorganized students. You may not know how to begin this type of assignment, or you get behind and not know how to make adjustments in your plan. The first step is to make an initial long-range plan. The next step is to adjust your plan when not everything goes as expected. The worst approach is to ignore the assignment until it is almost due, then rush through it, and not do a good job.

Number 5:

Many students look organized but are not! This is because their parents do all of the organizing for them. If you have too much help from your parents, you are not learning how to organize on your own. One strategy that works well is for your family to get a large household calendar and ask everyone in the household to write their own activities on the calendar. Use a different color pen for each person. This will help you learn to think ahead about your plans, and take a first step in responsibility.

Number 6 & 7:

Leaving items at home is a habit that can be broken if there is a consequence for not having these items at school. Students should not be constantly "rescued" by their parents. Gather up everything the night before and place it all in a container near the door. This may take up an inordinate amount of time at night, but it eliminates your morning scramble. Double-check to make sure you aren't forgetting anything.

Number 8:

This is the personal calendar question. Learn to carry a small calendar to write down important dates. Start by writing down your own birthday on your calendar. Carrying a visual reminder of time, whether it is a paper calendar or a hand-held computerized version, is an essential skill for all of us in the 21st century.

Number 9:

This is a question about distractions you face when you try to study. Our world has so many things that distract all of us, and it is more difficult to concentrate. Concentration is a habit we develop. Get a small timer. Find out how long you can concentrate without interruption. This is your baseline. Set the timer for one minute over your baseline. Usually students can push themselves to concentrate for one more minute. Continue to concentrate on not being distracted for a minute over your baseline each time you study. Do this for 21 days. In 21 days, this additional minute will be your new baseline. Then you can repeat the procedure adding another minute. Using this method over several months, you can increase your concentration.

Number 10:

This is the motivation question. If you answered "YES" to this question, you are motivated and ready to learn good organizational skills.

To find out more about ways you can improve your organizational skills, look at the numbers referenced on the next few pages. The numbers match the numbers on the Organization Quiz and target specific things you can do in each area.

No. 1, 6, 7

A Checklist of Supplies

Develop a checklist of the supplies you need for doing homework at home and supplies you need for your classes at school. Keep this list where you can see it often. You may decide to keep it on a wall in your room or even on the refrigerator door. You may want to change it every week or every grading period. An example is below.

School Supplies Checklist

Supplies needed at school:
___notebook paper
___2 pencils
___pen
___text for each class
___looseleaf notebook
___graph paper
___colored pencils
___calculator

Supplies needed at home:
___notebook paper
___pencil
___pen
___textbooks if assigned
___computer
___dictionary
___ruler
___phone numbers of smart/
responsible classmates

Think About It!

— What other supplies do you need at school?

your brain

What other things do you need in order to complete your homework assignments?

quiet place to work

On the next page make your own School Supplies Checklist.

SCHOOL SUPPLIES CHECKLIST

Items Needed at School -
Textbooks for Homework in:

Supplies

Items Needed at Home -
Textbooks in these subjects:

Supplies

Special homework papers in:

Notebooks for these subjects:

Other items:

Important phone numbers:
Name

Phone Number

Important Stuff

Reproducible page for student use.

No. 3, 4, 5, 8, 9

Calendars, "To Do" Lists, and Assignment Sheets

Most achievers learn how to schedule and manage their time well. Kids (and adults, too) have found that good time management is an important factor in achieving goals and in doing the things they really want to do. Working toward your goals is similar to building a house. Just as a hammer and saw might be tools you could use to build a house, calendars, "To Do" lists, and assignment sheets are time management and **organizational tools** that you can use.

Like any type of tool, using these to their best benefit takes practice. Most people can't use a hammer or saw perfectly the first time they pick one up, and most people have to **practice** using time management and organizational tools, too.

Sometimes kids think it takes too long to write things down, but writing things down actually saves time in the long run because it helps to organize your time. There are several advantages to these time management tools:

Calendars –

Calendars organize our time by days, weeks, months, and years. Most people write down their **scheduled activities** on a calendar; that is, the activities they need to attend that occur at a certain time. Some activities on the calendar may happen at the same time each week, like a Scout meeting. Others may only happen once, like a special musical production at school or a championship softball game.

Calendars are the tools we use to help us get to these events on the right day and at the right time! They also keep us from scheduling two things at the same time. You have probably noticed that it is hard to be in two places at once!!! People who use calendars are more organized because they have **control of their schedules**. People who don't use calendars tend to be disorganized. They often forget appointments or assignments and find they are supposed to be in two places at once, which is impossible to do.

SUNDAY	MONDAY	TUESDAY	WEDNESDAY	THURSDAY	FRIDAY	SATURDAY

Some people have very small calendars, which they carry in a pocket or purse, while others have larger ones that are more the size of a notebook or book. There are also palm pilots, hand-held organizers, and other computerized calendars you can use. Some cell phones have calendars as well. Try different types and find one that you like best.

You may want to copy and use the blank monthly calendar on the next page.

60

SUNDAY	MONDAY	TUESDAY	WEDNESDAY	THURSDAY	FRIDAY	SATURDAY

"To Do" Lists –

"To Do" Lists are simply lists of things you need to accomplish, but you do not have to do them at an exact time or on a specific date. For instance, filling out a college application would be something to put on a "To Do" List because you can do it any time until its deadline. Most things on a "To Do" List have deadlines (a date when they have to be completed), so an important part of using a "To Do" List is to plan **when** you will do the things that you write on your list.

Some people write their "To Do" Lists in order of **importance**, so that the first thing on the list is the most important thing to do. Other people put an 'A' beside items that have to be done right away, a 'B' beside items which should be done soon, and a 'C' beside the least important items.

Some people write a "To Do" List every day, some write it every week, and some just keep adding to it until they run out of space and have to start a new one. On the next pages, you will find "To Do" List forms you may want to use. There are two kinds of "To Do" Lists for you to use on pages 63 and 64 depending on your learning style. See how these forms work for you, or invent your own.

Assignment Sheets –

Assignment sheets are a special kind of "To Do" List designed specifically for students. They give you a place to write the subject, the assignment, and when it is due. The one in this book also gives you a place to note the materials you need to complete the assignment, and it gives you space to write four separate assignments on the same page. Make copies of this "Assignments To Do" page and use it for awhile. It will fit into your notebook, and you can throw it away when you've finished the listed assignments. Many students think it really helps them to organize their homework assignments. Try it! It is a good tool to use in becoming an achiever.

Another tool is the **"Long-Range Assignment Planning Guide"** on pages 66 and 67. It is an assignment sheet designed specifically to help you plan those projects that take a week or more to complete. There are two different kinds of guides depending on your learning style. You may want to list things in order (p. 66). Or you may want to list everything and then put them in order (p. 67). Use it the next time your teacher assigns a big project.

NEVER INTERUPT SOMEONE
DOING SOMETHING
YOU SAID COULDN'T BE DONE

AMELIA EARHART

"TO DO" LIST

Check When Completed	Activity	When I Plan To DO IT	Priority
_____ 1.	_____	1. _____	_____
	_____		
	_____		
_____ 2.	_____	2. _____	_____
	_____		
	_____		
_____ 3.	_____	3. _____	_____
	_____		
	_____		
_____ 4.	_____	4. _____	_____
	_____		
	_____		
_____ 5.	_____	5. _____	_____
	_____		
	_____		
_____ 6.	_____	6. _____	_____
	_____		
	_____		
_____ 7.	_____	7. _____	_____
	_____		
	_____		
_____ 8.	_____	8. _____	_____
	_____		
	_____		

Reproducible page for student use.

"TO DO" MINDMAP

Put the name of the day or identify the week in the middle circle. Write activities you need to do in each circle. Write the due date on the line.

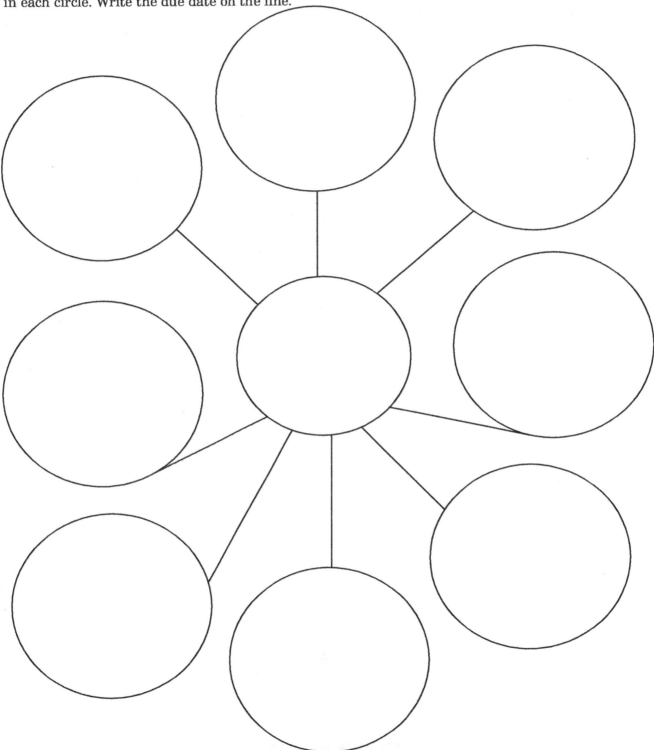

Reproducible page for student use.

© Pieces of Learning

ASSIGNMENTS TO DO

Today's Date: _____

Subject: _____

Assignment: _____

Materials Needed: _____

Due Tomorrow   Due Next Week   Due (Date)

_____   _____   _____

Subject:_____

Assignment: _____

Materials Needed: _____

Due Tomorrow   Due Next Week   Due (Date)

_____   _____   _____

Subject:_____

Assignment: _____

Materials Needed: _____

Due Tomorrow   Due Next Week   Due (Date)

_____   _____   _____

Subject: _____

Assignment:_____

Materials Needed: _____

Due Tomorrow   Due Next Week   Due (Date)

_____   _____   _____

Reproducible page for student use.

© Pieces of Learning

LONG-RANGE ASSIGNMENT PLANNING GUIDE

Topic/Project: _____

Expectations/Criteria:

_____

Steps to Completion   Target Date

1. _____

2. _____

3. _____

4. _____

5. _____

6. _____

7. _____

8. _____

Resources:

Reproducible page for student use.

LONG-RANGE ASSIGNMENT PLANNING GUIDE

Put the steps to completion in each circle. Write the target date on the lines.

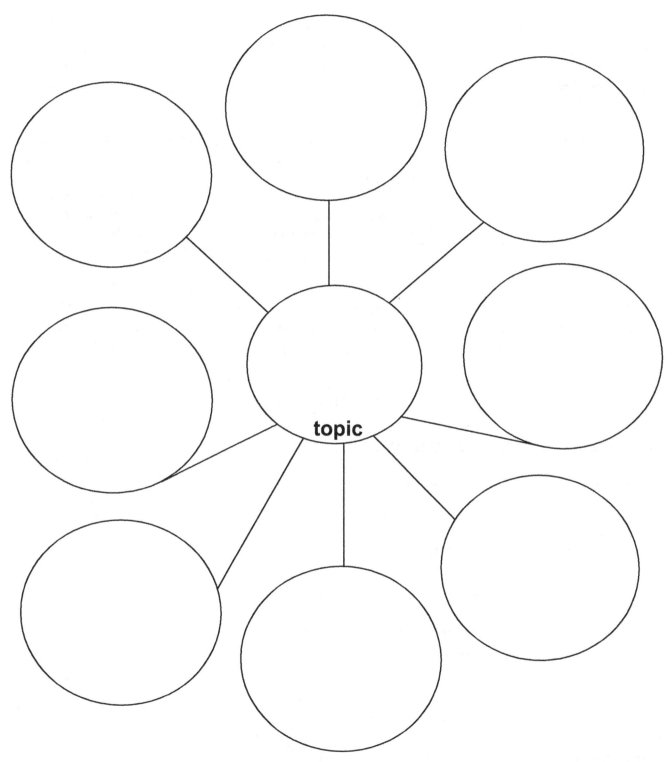

Reproducible page for student use.

No. 1, 2, 9

Organizing Your Notebooks

In general, everyone who goes to school has a collection of notes, notebook papers, handouts from teachers, test papers, homework papers, etc. that are supposed to be organized in some way. You may have a teacher who tells you exactly which papers you need to keep and exactly how to organize them. Other teachers just expect you to keep track of everything and have all of it when it is time to study for a test or turn in a project.

The easiest way to organize all of these papers is to have one large 3-ring notebook with dividers or several smaller different-colored notebooks so that you have one for each subject. Choosing different colors helps you remember which notebook is which subject (when you don't want to carry them all to class!) There are advantages and disadvantages to each. If you use a large notebook, you will be able to keep everything in one place. However, over the entire school year it may be too filled or too heavy. The smaller notebooks help you keep your subjects organized separately, but keeping track of them may be difficult. If your school has interdisciplinary studies, you may want to organize your notebooks by themes or projects instead of subjects.

The most important thing is to have a notebook system that works for you. The worst thing you can do is to continually throw all of your papers into the bottom of your locker, backpack, car, or closet and think that somehow you will be able to find the paper you need at the right time!

Think About It!

Describe your present system of organization.

very organized - I use separate binders for each subject

What changes would you like to make?

not having so many notebooks to keep track of

When will you make them?

Put a big X here_____ when you have made those changes.

5. Study Skills

Janelle, a 10th grader, described a typical day: "I get up at 6:15 and arrive at school by 7:10. When school is out at 2:45, I go to a Student Government meeting or another club and then to my part-time job. When I get home around 9:00, I'm tired, but I try to do a half hour or so of homework. I also like to talk to my friends on the phone, and some nights I just want to relax, so I guess I don't study very much. I usually do my written homework at lunch or in homeroom, and I get mostly B's and C's on my report card."

Are You Willing to Study?

Janelle is an active student in her school. Her teachers like her, and they praise her for her involvement in school activities. Yet many of them say she is not **"working up to her potential"** as a student. The biggest reason is that Janelle has not developed good study skills, nor has she put studying as a priority in her life. Other things like her activities, her job, and her friends come first.

Janelle is typical of many American students. Compared to other advanced countries of the world, achievement in U.S. schools appears less important than social life, extra curricular activities and part-time jobs. We seem to have the ideal of the "well rounded student" who is involved in sports, hobbies, community service, and after school jobs, but this schedule leaves very little time for serious study.

This approach may have worked in the past. However, in the 21st Century you are competing globally with countries all over the world. To be successful and competitive there needs to be an emphasis on studying.

It's not easy! Studying takes effort and discipline. This means choosing to study rather than doing another activity that may be more enjoyable. Students who study little learn little. Achievers are students who are **willing to study**, and, in the process, learn a great deal.

The first thing you must do to improve your study skills is to make up your mind that you are **willing** to put some time and effort into studying. Once you have made that decision, this chapter will show you **how to study** more effectively.

Reading

Reading is the most basic of all study skills. Most of your homework and studying involves reading in some way, but you may never have thought about what reading involves. It is a complex process! First, reading involves **decoding**. That is the process of looking at a word, sounding it out, and saying it, either silently to yourself (silent reading) or out loud (oral reading). In the early grades of elementary school, students spend a lot of time learning to decode words.

Some students have a hard time decoding nearly all of the words in their reading assignments. If you fall into this category, you may need to work with a special teacher or tutor to build up your reading skills.

Most students, however, can read most of the words in their assignments, but have trouble with **new** vocabulary words. These words seem to be a problem particularly when they read about new topics. Many kids skip over the words they don't know, because they can finish the assignment faster. But this defeats the purpose of doing the reading in the first place!

Surprisingly, if you learn and understand the new vocabulary, you will generally learn and understand the whole topic you are studying. The vocabulary tends to be like a key that opens the door to whatever the topic is.

Therefore, a good reading strategy is to look up the meanings of unfamiliar words — **as you read.** Or skim the assignment first for new words and write down the meanings. Then use the list to help you as you read.

Have you ever read an assignment and then when you finished you couldn't remember one word you had read? Nearly everyone has experienced this at one time or another. When it happens, your brain is decoding the words, (therefore you are "reading") but you are not concentrating enough to think about and remember what you've read.

How can you concentrate? These ideas can help you:

1. Distractions –Try eliminating people who are talking, certain kinds of music, and TV.
2. Room arrangement – Use good lighting so you don't tire your eyes; position your body so it is not an invitation to take a nap!
3. Timing – Don't wait until the last minute to read an assignment when your mind is on "not enough time" rather than on the assignment.
4. Write down mental distractions if you have them. Then you have less to clutter your mind.
5. If you own the book from which you are reading, try highlighting or underlining important words, facts, or ideas.

THE BOTTOM LINE IS MAKE A DECISION TO CONCENTRATE AND DO IT!

If you understand the vocabulary, and if you learn to concentrate, this leads to being able to do the next part of the reading process, **comprehension**. It involves the ability to understand what you are reading. The most important elements in comprehension are **thinking** and **remembering**. A student who thinks about what he or she is reading and then remembers it afterwards has mastered the most basic study skill.

Think About It!

You might say you need to have your brain in gear before you start to read! List what makes reading your assignments difficult for you. Do you read without thinking? Do you daydream? Do you procrastinate?

Write 2 things you could do to improve how you read and study.

1. focus - don't draw your attention away to someone or something

2. read the whole passage through; don't stop to do something else. 1 thing at a time

Learning What You Read

Make several copies of "Learning What You Read" on page 72 so you can use it each time you have a reading assignment. It has a place for you to put new vocabulary words with short definitions, a place for main ideas, and a place for important facts. Using it as you read not only will help your concentration and memory, it will also give you an excellent study sheet to use before a test!

What's The Right Speed?

The page entitled **"What's The Right Speed...How Fast Should You Read?"** compares reading to driving a car. Did you know that you read at different speeds depending on the type of things you are reading and the types of assignments you have?

Sometimes you can read very quickly, like a "Speed Demon." But at other times, you have to read more slowly, like you're "Cruisin' Through McDonald's®" or driving over speed bumps. Use page 73 to help you know how fast you should read for each assignment.

LEARNING WHAT YOU READ

Subject _____

Book/Pages _____

Vocabulary Words	Short Definition
1. _____	1. _____
2. _____	2. _____
3. _____	3. _____
4. _____	4. _____
5. _____	5. _____
6. _____	6. _____
7. _____	7. _____
8. _____	8. _____
9. _____	9. _____
10. _____	10. _____

Main Ideas/Important Concepts:

Facts to Remember:

Reproducible page for student use.

WHAT'S THE RIGHT SPEED...How Fast Should You Read?

Like driving, people read at different speeds, depending on the circumstances.

"Speed Demon" (Skimming)
1000-2000 words per minute
-To locate a specific reference or vocabulary word
-To find the answer to a specific question
-To get an overview of a chapter, short story, or article

"Interstate Travel" (Very Rapid Reading)
500-1000 words per minute
-To review something you have already read
-To read magazines, comic books, or feature articles in newspapers
-To read for pleasure, for example an easy novel

"Driving in Town" (Rapid Reading)
350-500 words per minute
Fiction:
-To read fiction that is somewhat difficult
-To read for characterization, theme, mood, imagery
Non-Fiction:
-To find the main idea and make generalizations
-To understand patterns and sequence

"Cruisin' Through McDonald's®" (Moderate Reading)
250-350 words per minute
Fiction:
-To read complex fiction for characterization, plot analysis; to understand relationships between characters and ideas
Non-Fiction:
-To note details, compare and contrast information, distinguish between fact and opinion

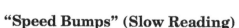

"Speed Bumps" (Slow Reading)
100-250 words per minute
Fiction:
-To evaluate quality and literary merit
Non-Fiction:
-To study and master content, including facts and details
-To read technical or scientific material
-To solve a complex problem
-To follow detailed directions
-To translate from another language

Reproducible page for student use.

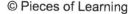

Juan is an average 6th grade student whose achievement tests show that he could be doing much better than he is. When he began middle school, he realized that he couldn't remember all of the information from the lectures and class discussions. He talked to his friends about it to see if they were having the same problem. Some of them said they took notes during class and reminded Juan that the teachers had talked to them about note taking.

"How can I listen and write at the same time?" Juan asked. "Besides, I don't know what to write. It's impossible to write down everything they say!"

Juan could become an achiever if he developed good listening and note taking skills.

Listening and Note Taking

You may feel the same way Juan does when it comes to taking notes in class. You may think that the best thing to do in class is to listen and try to remember everything in your head. The problem with that is there is just too much to remember!

When you take notes, you can look back to see what has been said. Your notes help when you study for tests. And…one great way to add new information into your brain is to write it down. Amazingly, just the act of writing helps your brain learn new information!

In becoming an achiever and developing good study skills, learning how to listen and take good notes is extremely important. This is especially true when you have a teacher who spends a lot of time lecturing. Follow the suggestions for good note taking and good listening on the next two pages to improve your skills.

ALL THINGS ARE
DIFFICULT
BEFORE THEY ARE
EASY

Suggestions for Good Note Taking

1. Come to class prepared.
Look over other class notes and read the assigned textbook pages. The lecture will make much more sense if you have some background about what the teacher said. Figure out how today's lecture relates to what was said yesterday.

2. Concentrate on **what** is being said **not how it is said** or **not who** is saying it.
There are some teachers you like more than others. Don't let this affect how well you listen in class. Even a teacher you dislike may have valuable information to give you!

3. Keep mentally and physically alert.
Get enough sleep and eat breakfast before coming to school. You think you don't have time to eat breakfast, but your body needs fuel to get through the day. Take time to eat something in the morning. Do you have trouble staying awake in class? Go to bed a half hour earlier. Getting enough sleep makes a tremendous difference in your ability to concentrate!

4. Listen, think, and write.
You can do all three of these at the same time! Most teachers speak at the rate of approximately 100 words per minute. Most people can think at about 400 words per minute. Use the time to think about what is really important to write down.

5. Try to focus on the main idea.
What seems to be the main point or points the teacher is emphasizing? You may want to write them down. If you are not sure, ask the teacher!

6. Write the teacher's examples in your notes.
Many kids think that when the teacher is giving an example, this is the time they don't have to pay attention. Not true! Examples often turn into test items. Pay attention to them and write them down.

7. Ask yourself, "What would I ask on a test from this information?"
Write your sample test questions at the end of your notes. Giving yourself a test is a great way to study. Trade your test with a study partner. Do you both anticipate the same questions? Are there surprises?

8. Make a list, highlight, or underline those things the teacher said that are completely new to you.
These are the things you will have to review and learn, because you don't already know them. Skim the rest of the lecture notes for a quick review before the test.

Checklist for Good Listening

☐ I gave the speaker my complete attention.

☐ I concentrated on what the speaker was saying.

☐ I didn't argue mentally with the speaker even when I disagreed with what he or she was saying.

☐ I kept my brain in gear and didn't daydream during the talk.

☐ I didn't make snap judgments about what the speaker was saying.

☐ I looked at the speaker when he or she was talking.

☐ I watched the speaker's non-verbal communication AND listened to what the speaker said.

☐ I asked appropriate questions.

☐ I paid enough attention to be able to write down key ideas about what the speaker said. (Write below.)

☐ I was able to find connections between my own ideas and knowledge and the ideas and knowledge of the speaker. (Write below.)

Key ideas:

Connections to my own knowledge and ideas:

Reproducible form for student use.

How to Tell What is Important

It's impossible to write down every word that is said in class. Even if you could do it, you wouldn't want to! It's not a very effective way to learn. And writing down everything wouldn't necessarily help you understand the material.

In an average day at school, most of your time is spent listening to your teachers and other classmates. Good listening skills involve knowing what is important and what is not. As you take notes, you may find it very difficult to know what you should write down. There are a number of ways to find out. Try the suggestions below and see which work best for you.

You can tell that something is important when the teacher:
- Changes his/her tone of voice
- Puts something on the chalkboard
- Uses an illustration or example
- Gives you a formula or diagram
- Pauses so that you have time to write
- Repeats the same point
- Slows down for emphasis

You can tell that something is important when the teacher <u>says</u>:
- Note this…
- The four main points are…
- This is important…
- You'll probably see this again…
- Make sure you remember this…
- This type of thing is on the (SAT, Achievement Test, etc.) …

_____ Your teacher's favorite phrase

Think About It!

Think about how you take notes.

Which of the above suggestions have you already noticed in class?

_____

_____

Which will you try? In what class?

_____

_____

Memorization Techniques

Tommy always understands the main concepts and ideas of his school subjects. He loves class discussion and can usually win arguments with people. However, Tommy can never remember the facts. He can't remember names or places or dates in history; he can't remember scientific names in biology; and he can't remember formulas in math. He does poorly on tests because he doesn't study the facts and details he needs to know. He needs to learn some memorization techniques.

Learning how to memorize important information is a basic study skill. A few people have "photographic memories" and can memorize things just by looking at them. But most of us aren't like that. Most of us have trouble memorizing things and have to work at it. If you have trouble memorizing, you need to learn some special memorization techniques.

1. Relate the facts that you need to memorize to something you **already know**.
Anything is easier to learn when it can be related to something you already know. Sometimes one fact will relate to another very easily. For instance, if you know that Ohio and West Virginia border one another, it is easy to remember that the Ohio River separates the two. Sometimes things don't relate to one another very well, but you can make up a funny saying to help you remember. For instance, if you need to remember that frogs are amphibians, you may make up a funny story about a frog named Amphy!

2. Use **mnemonic devices** to help you remember things. These are types of formulas that make things easier to remember.

3. Use **acronyms**. Make a word or phrase from the first letter of each word you need to learn.
Example:
If you need to learn the names of the lines on a music staff (**EGBDF**) you can remember
Every **G**ood **B**oy **D**oes **F**ine

4. Make up a **rhyme, song, or poem** containing the information you need to memorize.
Example:
In fourteen hundred and ninety-two,
Columbus sailed the ocean blue.

5. Use the **"Location Method."**
Picture the words you need to memorize on **objects in a familiar room**. To remember them, mentally walk around the room, locating them one by one.

6. Visualize mentally the things you need to memorize.

7. Make note of **examples** in order to remember abstract ideas.
Abstract idea = conflict
Your example = fight with your brother

8. Organize information into **categories**. It is easier to remember small pieces of information when we place them in a larger category.
Generally, we can remember seven to ten items in this way. That's why most of us can remember our phone numbers, social security numbers, and even our extended zip codes!
Example:
To memorize the 13 original colonies, put them in categories according to their geographical location:

North
Massachusetts
New Hampshire
Rhode Island
Connecticut
New York

Central
Maryland
New Jersey
Delaware
Pennsylvania

South
Virginia
North Carolina
South Carolina
Georgia

9. Use **flow charts** and other **visual organizers** to help you see how information is organized and how facts and ideas relate to one another.
Example:

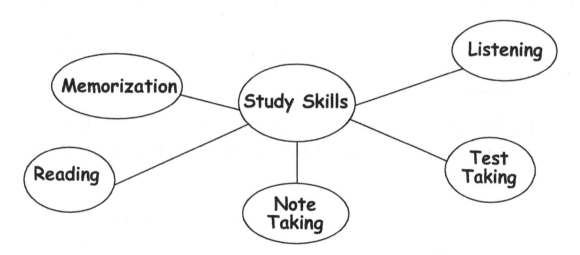

10. Use a **study guide** or **outline** of the things you need to know.
Try to pinpoint the most important concepts and facts in the lesson. Make an outline or study guide to help you know which things are the most important.

11. Put the main ideas or concepts you need to learn on **index cards**.
Write the main idea or concept on one side of the card and supporting facts on the other. This will help you organize information because you can arrange the cards in categories, which makes memorization easier. Use index cards as flashcards to memorize vocabulary, facts, or terms you need to know.

Think About It!

What are the best ways for you to memorize information?

_____

_____

Write down the memorization techniques you use.

_____

_____

List those you would like to try.

_____

_____

Which subjects do you find most difficult in terms of memorization? Why?

_____

_____

Talk to the teacher about your problems. Decide on a plan for improving your skills in memorizing the vocabulary and/or concepts for that class. Write your plan in the space below.

_____

_____

_____

_____

_____

STUDY SKILLS ASSESSMENT

Rate yourself in each of the following study skills using the scale below.

1 = I almost always do this   3 = I use this skill occasionally

2 = I use this skill most of the time   4 = I almost never use this skill

_____ 1. I follow written directions.

_____ 2. I follow oral directions.

_____ 3. I listen and I understand what is being said.

_____ 4. I take notes when I listen to a lesson or lecture.

_____ 5. I take notes when I read the text or other written material.

_____ 6. I understand the material when I do reading assignments.

_____ 7. I keep my belongings well organized.

_____ 8. I can find my assignments after I have completed them.

_____ 9. I manage my time well.

_____ 10. I plan the steps in doing long-range assignments.

_____ 11. I know several good memorization techniques.

_____ 12. I know how to preview a chapter in a textbook.

_____ 13. I know how to study vocabulary in any subject area.

_____ 14. I set short-term goals.

_____ 15. I set long-term goals.

_____ 16. I can concentrate on what I'm supposed to be studying.

_____ 17. I work without interruptions.

_____ 18. I can write an organized paragraph.

_____ 19. I proofread my written work.

_____ 20. I know how to use many different sources in research.

_____ 21. I use the Internet when I do research.

_____ 22. I take notes from many sources when I do research.

_____ 23. I know how to read and produce maps, charts, and graphs.

_____ 24. I know how to study for an objective or selected response test.

_____ 25. I know how to study for an essay or constructed response test.

_____ 26. I can produce a project or product that shows what I know.

Look at the items you scored 1 or 2. Which study skills are you best in?
Look at the items you scored 3 or 4. Which study skills need improvement?

Taken from *Solving the Assessment Puzzle* by Coil & Merritt
Web site: www.piecesoflearning.com

Reproducible page for student use.

Finding Academic Holes

Batina has made it to fourth grade, but sometimes she feels lost in class. The worst time of the day is during math. The teacher thinks that she should be working on decimals and fractions. The problem is that Batina really doesn't know her multiplication facts very well, especially the 7's, 8's, and 9's. The teacher has told her that she is intelligent and should be doing well in math, but each day she falls further and further behind.

Batina has a great sense of humor, and a lot of her friends are in her class, so she now clowns around in class. This has not been a very good idea, because her teacher now thinks of Batina as a behavior problem.

Jason is a sixth grader. He made it through elementary school getting B's and C's on his report card. His parents and teachers knew he could do better because he didn't study very much in elementary school. At the beginning of the school year, he entered middle school. He was placed in an advanced class because he was smart, but most of his teachers can see that he has problems. He can't write his thoughts in complete sentences, doesn't know how to learn the scientific terms taught in science class, and fails math tests because he doesn't know basic math facts. However, he's good in class discussion, has advanced knowledge of current events, and enjoys talking to his science teacher about conservation and the environment. When Jason received his first middle school report card, he received C's and D's.

Batina and Jason could be achievers if they would identify and work to improve their "academic holes."

What Are Academic Holes?

Have you ever had a hole in your pocket? If you have, you know that even a small hole can be annoying and inconvenient. Somehow things keep slipping through. Or think of an email address with one letter missing. Even though all the rest of it is there, the email just won't go through.

It's the same way with your brain and the knowledge it has stored. Perhaps in one of the early grades of elementary school, you never listened to the teacher and therefore missed several important basic concepts in science. Or you could have been daydreaming through an important class discussion in English.

Many students have "holes" in their academic skills. This means there are things that they should have learned, but for one reason or another, they did not. You may not be aware that you have this problem. Academic holes are as annoying as holes in your pockets or email addresses that don't work. They make it much more difficult to do your assignments and do them well.

There are ways to patch the academic holes so that the most marvelous computer of all (your brain) works exactly as it should!

Think About It!

Most students know what their academic holes are without having to go through any formalized testing. Just as you know your strengths, you also know your trouble spots.

Write three academic holes you believe you have.

_____

_____

_____

You have now taken the first step in patching your academic holes! You have identified what they are. There are several other ways to identify academic holes or weaknesses. You can ask your teacher in which areas he or she thinks you have the most problems. You can request a special kind of testing called **diagnostic testing** to help you see what you need to work on. You can look back at papers you have done in the past and see what types of mistakes you always seem to make. You may discover a pattern, which would lead you to discover an academic hole.

Another way to find academic holes is to have an understanding of how your school's curriculum is organized. Most schools have the day divided up into a number of different subjects areas. You may have reading, language arts, math, science, etc. Each week these subjects take up a certain amount of time per day or per week. If your school divides the day by subjects, and there is one part of the day that is more difficult for you than the others, then you have a good clue about your academic hole. But be careful! Many students will just say, *"Oh I can't do math!"* or *"I'm no good at history,"* when it is just a small portion of the subject that they don't do well, not the entire subject.

Another way your studies may be organized is by thematic units. This is sometimes called interdisciplinary studies. What this means is that you and your classmates study a large topic or theme (like the Middle Ages) and all of the subjects are interrelated and taught as a part of that theme. Many times students working in cooperative learning groups study these units. If you are part of a cooperative learning group, the people in your group can help you identify and work on some of your academic weaknesses. In a group situation, though, be careful not to let someone else always do the part of the assignment that is hard for you. If you do, you'll never learn how to do it yourself!

Once you have found academic holes, the next step is to make a plan for filling them. The plan could be to…

…work with a special tutor

…get extra help from your teacher

…find a peer tutor

…pay closer attention to your weak areas

Most of us enjoy working on things we are good at, and we tend to avoid the things we don't do very well. Most likely you have tried to avoid the subject or skill in which you have academic holes.

In the world of sports, however, things don't work that way. If an athlete finds a weak area, he usually works harder on that area in order to build it up. That is the area which will receive the most attention and practice. The same should be true for academic weaknesses. Your plan of action should concentrate on finding a way to build up the weaknesses that you have.

Think About It!

Think about a plan of action to help plug your academic holes.

Filling out the form on the next page should help guide your thinking.

**ATTEMPT THE IMPOSSIBLE
IN ORDER TO IMPROVE
YOUR WORK**

BETTE DAVIS

ACADEMIC HOLES PLAN OF ACTION FORM

Subject Area _____

Specific "Academic Holes" (Be as detailed as possible)

_____

_____

_____

_____

Things I could do to improve my skills and plug these holes (List as many as you can think of)

1. _____

2. _____

3. _____

4. _____

5. _____

6. _____

7. _____

My Plan:
Circle the ideas you will try in the next week.

Share these ideas with a teacher, parent, friend, peer tutor, or mentor.

Reproducible page for student use.

6. Tests and Other Assessments

Maria is a fifth grader who doesn't do very well on tests. She does her homework papers neatly and correctly, and she usually has pretty good ideas when the class has discussions. She tends to be a perfectionist and puts a great deal of pressure on herself to do well in school. In fact, she thinks she spends lots of time studying for tests, but much of her study time is spent worrying about how hard the test is going to be. When it actually is time to take the test, Maria gets very nervous, and then when she receives poor grades on test papers, she gets really upset. Maria could be an excellent student, but she suffers from 'test anxiety' and has poor test taking skills.

Test Taking

Tests are receiving lots of attention in schools. Both students and their teachers are under a great deal of pressure to do well. Tests can be the deciding factor in whether you will pass to the next grade or even if you will graduate from high school.

"High stakes" tests are tests that are extremely important in deciding your future. These might be standardized tests given near the end of the school year or college entrance exams like the PSAT, SAT or ACT.

You probably take lots of other tests, too. Usually teachers give tests at the end of a unit of study. Some teachers give weekly tests or even daily quizzes. Sometimes you may have to take a pretest so that the teacher can learn how much you already know about a topic before she begins teaching.

In all of these cases, it is important to have excellent test taking skills.

Believe it or not, knowing how to take a test is just as important as knowing the information that is on it! Like Maria, there are many people who experience a certain kind of stress called "test anxiety" when they have to take a test. People who have test anxiety do not do well on tests, even though they may know most of the answers. This is because they are so nervous before and during the test, they don't think very clearly.

There are a number of other reasons that people have trouble with tests. Some students have not learned to manage their time well during the test itself. Perhaps you have taken a test where you knew the answers, but you didn't have time to finish. Perhaps you remember a time when you got stuck on one question, and this negatively affected you for the rest of the test.

Some kids are poor test takers because they rush through the test without reading the directions or without reading the questions carefully. Have you ever done an entire test incorrectly because you didn't bother to read the directions? Or perhaps you thought the question was asking one thing, but when you got it back and read the question again, you saw that it was really asking something else. Whatever your problems have been in test taking, the next few pages should help you with them.

Think About It!

List a problem you have had taking tests.

_____

_____

_____

List a test taking problem area you want to improve.

_____

_____

_____

_____

_____

_____

_____

_____

A TEST ABOUT TESTS

Or... Do You Have Test Anxiety?

Scoring: 4 – This describes me exactly.
                            3 – This describes the way I usually feel.
                            2 – Sometimes I feel like this.
                            1 – I rarely feel this way.
                            0 – I have never felt like this.

_____1. I never feel prepared when I take a test.

_____2. I start to feel physically nervous and stressed before a test is given.

_____3. I can guarantee that I will not do well on any test I take.

_____4. The computerized test answer sheets tend to confuse me.

_____5. When I come across a question that I don't know, I panic.

_____6. I panic when others finish a test before I do, even if it's not a timed test.

_____7. I have mental blocks when I am taking a test.

_____8. I worry that I will run out of time during a timed test.

_____9. I look around the room and feel that everyone else taking the test knows more than I do.

_____10. The word "test" makes me panic.

_____TOTAL

Score Interpretation

40-31 You suffer from major test anxiety. Stress reduction techniques, a time management plan, working to build your self-confidence, and learning a variety of study skills will help.

30-21 You have problems in test taking which are due to test anxiety. Relaxation techniques before a test and using a variety of study skills will help.

20-11 You are usually relaxed in your approach to test taking. It would be helpful to pinpoint any items that you scored a 3 or 4.

10 or Below You have little if any test anxiety!

Reproducible page for student use.

Test Taking Hints for Students

TIME MANAGEMENT

1. Look over the entire exam **first**. Notice **how many** questions are on the test and **how long** you have to take the test.

Note the number of sections or questions and estimate how much time you will have to spend on each item. Try to adjust your speed to match the time allotted for the questions.

2. Take into account the **weighting** or number of points each item or section of the test is worth.

You may want to start with questions other than the first one. It will depend upon how much each item is worth.

3. Bring a watch to help you keep track of the **time** and judge your **speed** as you take the exam. You may need to adjust your speed.

4. Don't spend **too much time** on any one item.

If you can't decide between two or three choices, go ahead and choose one. If there is no penalty for guessing, this is always the best approach. Mark the question on your paper in some way if you think you might want to go back to it if you have time.

5. **Do not rush** to get through the test.

Use all the time you are given. **There are no extra points given for being the first to finish!**

6. Find out if you are penalized for **guessing.**

If you are not, when you see your time is almost up and you have not answered all the questions, fill in answers at random for all the unanswered questions. You will not have time to read the questions when you do this, but guessing at random is better than no answer at all.

Test Taking Hints for Students

FOLLOWING DIRECTIONS

1. **Listen** carefully to oral directions.

Some tests are designed so that the person giving the test is required to read a certain set of directions. Listen carefully and read along with the printed directions on the test.

2. Look for **key words** in the directions.

Sometimes the directions will tell you to work only to a certain item number, or not to turn over your test booklet, or to do all items except for certain ones. Be sure you are aware of key words.

3. **Follow all written and oral directions** for taking the test and marking the answer sheet. Know exactly **how to record** your answers.

Are you supposed to write in the test booklet? Must you use a certain type of pencil? Do you mark + for True and 0 for False? Pay close attention to the directions to learn these things. Be careful how you mark your answers! Particularly with computerized score sheets, answers have to be marked in a certain way or they do not count.

4. Pay attention to the **sample item** or items in the directions.

Many tests have sample questions. Look at them to get an idea about how the questions should be answered.

OBSTACLES ARE THOSE
FRIGHTFUL THINGS YOU SEE
WHEN YOU TAKE YOUR EYES
OFF THE GOAL

HENRY FORD

Think About It!

Have you made careless mistakes on tests because you didn't follow the directions?

What do you find most difficult to do in following directions on a test?

_____

_____

_____

_____

_____

List one way you can improve.

_____

_____

_____

_____

_____

_____

Test Taking Hints for Students

READING THE QUESTIONS

1. Ask yourself:

   What is this question **really** asking?

   Are there any **key words**?

   How would I **ask** this question in my own words?

   How would I **answer** this question in my own words?

2. Don't read things into the question that aren't there.

   ### Example
   Franklin Roosevelt was President of the United States in:
   - a. 1940
   - b. 1923
   - c. 1894
   - d. None of these

   If you know he was President in 1940 choose (a). Don't choose (d) thinking that (a) doesn't list all the years he was President. That would be reading something into the question that isn't there.

3. Don't make assumptions about details that are not stated.

   ### Example
   Prince Charles, the heir to the British throne, married:
   - a. Princess Grace
   - b. Princess Caroline
   - c. Princess Diana
   - d. None of these

   Even though Prince Charles and Princess Diana were divorced at the time of her death, choose (c). They did marry.

4. Be aware of you own biases. Do not base your answers solely on your personal beliefs or experiences.

   Example True or False: According to a recent Gallup survey, the number of courses offered in foreign language in school has increased in American schools as compared to 1963.

*If you and your friends have never taken a foreign language class, you may think this statement is false. If you and your friends have, you may think this statement is true. Remember, the question asks for the facts in a survey, not **your** opinion.*

5. Use your best logical reasoning and general knowledge.

Example

Environmental scientists consider which of the following as a threat to the environment in the 21st Century?
    a. oil spills
    b. air pollution
    c. over population
    d. all of the above

*Your general knowledge would help you on this question. Logically you would know that any of the choices given could be a threat to the environment. Also, if you know any **two** of the choices are correct, logic will tell you to choose (d).*

6. Read questions first in "reading passages." Circle the key words. Then read the passage and circle the key words in each sentence. It will help you to think about what you are reading, and then you can match the key words in the questions with the key words in the answer.

Example

What did jealous people try to do to these simple people?
    a. change their laws
    b. take over their island
    c. join the celebrations

In what ocean do these Polynesians live?
    a. Pacific Ocean
    b. Atlantic Ocean
    c. Indian Ocean
    d. Arctic Ocean

On a small Pacific island live many families of Polynesian descent. Mothers and fathers teach children to communicate with one another and barter for things they need and want. Everyone's birthday is a festival even after a hard day's work in the sugarcane fields. Their simple customs and traditions have lived through the decades despite the many times jealous neighboring islanders have attempted to take over their island.

Test Taking Hints for Students

CONSIDERING GRAMMAR AND WORDING

1. Look for **key words** such as **all, never, only, no, none, always**. These words usually make the statement false. Key words such as **somewhat, usually, most**, and **sometimes** generally make the statement true. Circle them if you are allowed to.

Example

Penguins are found in the wild (only) in Antarctica. (false)

(Most) penguins in the wild are found in Antarctica. (true)

2. Use clues such as **verb tense** and the use of **"an"** or **"a"** to reduce possible answers and save time. If the grammar in the question does not match the grammar in the answer, that answer is incorrect.

Example

A bird that does not fly is (an)
    a. robins
    b. parrot
    c. emu
    d. orioles

Eliminate **a** _because it is plural and does not begin with a vowel_
Eliminate **b** _because it does not begin with a vowel_
Eliminate **d** _because it is plural_
The answer is **c.**

3. Look for words in the answers that are **similar** to the words in the question.

Example

Chemicals that kill (insects) are called:

    a. biological controls

    b. bombers

    c. plankton

    d. insecticides

The word **"insecticide"** _is similar to the word insect._ **d** _is the correct answer._

4. Look for key words in the question that tell you exactly the kind of answer that is called for.

Example

List 3 causes of the Civil War.

Causes *is the key word. This is exactly what is being asked for. Don't list battles, generals, events, or results.*

5. Watch for chances to **use information** given in one question as clues to the answer to another question.

Example

1. The central mass of protoplasm in a cell is the:
    a. nucleus
    b. cell wall
    c. cell membrane
    d. cytoplasm

2. The nucleus in the center of the cell controls:
    a. tissues
    b. organs
    c. reproduction
    d. osmosis

Question #2 says that **nucleus** *is in the* **center of the cell**. *You can figure out that the answer to the first question is nucleus (a) by reading the other question.*

SUCCESS DOESN'T
HAPPEN TO YOU.
YOU MAKE
SUCCESS HAPPEN.

Test Taking Hints for Students

MULTIPLE CHOICE TESTS

Lots of the tests you take are multiple choice or selected response tests. That is, you have the question and then a series of answers to choose from. Most of the standardized achievement tests and college board tests are in this format because they are easy to score. But these kinds of questions can also be confusing. There are many ways to help yourself become more successful in taking this type of test.

1. Read each question carefully and consider all of the choices. If more than one answer seems correct, choose the **best** answer by making connections.

Example
The form of government in the United States is:
    a. dictatorship
    b. democracy
    c. theocracy
    d. capitalism

*You may know that the United States is a **democracy** and that our economic system is **capitalism**. Even though capitalism is tied closely to our government, the best choice is (b) because **democracy** more closely relates to **government** than to economy. The question asks about **government**.*

2. When three of the answers are very similar in meaning, **the other** answer is usually the correct one.

Example
A noun is:
    a. a word that shows action
    b. a word that expresses the doing of something
    c. a word that names a person, place, thing
    d. a word that shows movement

*Choices (b) "doing" and (d) "movement" are similar to (a) "action." The choice that has a **different** meaning is (c). That is the correct answer.*

3. When all of the answers are correct, choose the answer that includes all of the others.

Example
The following happened during the Vietnam War era:
    a. There were anti-war protests in Washington, D.C.
    b. Men were drafted.
    c. Students were killed at Kent State University.
    d. All of the above.

Because choices (a), (b), and (c) **are all correct**, *choose (d).*

4. If all of the answers except one seem correct, reread the beginning of the question. It may be asking for "all of these EXCEPT the following."

Example
All of the following happened during the Vietnam War era except:
    a. There were anit-war protests in Washington. D.C.
    b. Men were drafted.
    c. Women were drafted.
    d. Students were killed at Kent State University.

The correct answer is (c) because all of the other choices **did happen** *during the Vietnam era.*

5. If an answer has more than one part, look for parts that are incorrect. **If one part is incorrect**, the entire answer is incorrect. Cross out the incorrect choices.

Example
Two major parts of a sentence are:
    a. subject and ~~adjective~~
    b. ~~noun~~ and ~~adjective~~
    c. ~~adjective~~ and predicate
    d. subject and predicate

The correct choice is (d) because only **part** *of the other choices is correct.*

6. Circle **key words** in the question. Then formulate an answer **before** reading the answer choices. As you look at the given answers ask, "Is there an answer similar to the one I thought of? Is this the best answer of the choices given?"

Example

World War II ended in:
- a. 1940
- b. 1944
- c. 1945
- d. 1947

Before you look at the choices, decide what your answer is. If you think World War II ended in 1945, you are right! Look to see if that is one of the choices.

7. Some answers will seem incorrect, irrelevant, ridiculous, too general or too limited. **Eliminate these first** and you will have less possible answers from which to choose.

Example

A famous rock star born in Tupelo, Mississippi, in 1935:
- a. Elvis Presley
- b. The Beatles
- c. Justin Timberlake
- d. Bill Clinton

You can easily eliminate all of the incorrect choices from this question. The Beatles are a group, not one rock star. Justin Timberlake is much too young to have been born in 1935 (over 65 years ago!). And Bill Clinton is not a rock star (even though he plays the saxophone). He became President of the United States in the 1990's. Therefore, the correct answer is (a).

8. Which answer actually **sounds** the best? If there appear to be 2 correct answers, you can restate the question with an answer to see how it sounds.

**A MAN'S DREAMS
ARE AN INDEX
TO HIS GREATNESS**

Z. RABINWITZ

Test Taking Hints for Students

CONSTRUCTED RESPONSE QUESTIONS

Constructed responses are answers you have to think of and write on your own. Examples include essays or short answer exams that require thought and organization. On this type of test, you are usually given a rather broad question that you must answer by writing the information you know as well as your opinions and interpretations about it.

1. Budget your time. If there is more than one question, you will have to decide how long to spend on each. Which requires more thought? Which do you know? Which one is most difficult? Plan how much time you need or will use to write each answer.

2. Think through what you are going to write before you begin. List, outline, or make a web of your main points and jot down key words or phrases before you begin.

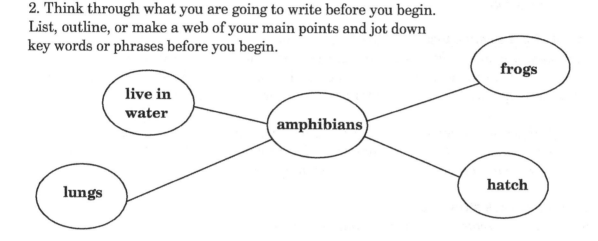

3. Begin by writing in general terms and then back up what you say by providing examples.

4. Begin a new paragraph for each main idea. Use your outline or web as a guide.

5. No matter what subject the essay exam is being written for, observe rules of correct English usage. Therefore, when you have finished writing, it is important to proofread your answers.

Check for:

• **Lack of clarity**
Are there any sentences in which your ideas seem muddled?

Example
Where do amphibians live?
> *Amphibians are animals that live on land and in water but sometimes they live in one place and sometimes they live in another just depending on their stage.*

It would be clearer if you said...

Amphibians are animals that begin their lives in the water. Later they develop lungs and live on the land.

- **False statements**

When re-reading your essay did you write anything you now know is not true or correct?

Example

Amphibians may be one-celled and reproduce through simple cell division.

After thinking about it, you may remember that frogs come from tadpoles that hatch from eggs. You would need to change your false statement. **Take the time to change it!**

- **Statements that are too vague or have no meaning**

Are there phrases or sentences that you included just to fill up space that really add nothing to what you are saying?

Example for a science test Describe Amphibians:

Amphibians are important in science, but the term is also used in the military for those things that can be used on the land or in the water. Amphibians have helped our military forces, especially in battles for islands in combat areas in oceans.

While this information may be interesting and may be something you could use in history, it doesn't add to a **science test** _about amphibians. The information will not increase your score. And you will be wasting your time!_

- **Incorrect sentence structure**

Do you have run-on sentences or phrases that are misplaced?

Example

Amphibians include a number of different animals such as frogs, toads, and salamanders that spend part of their lives on land and part of their lives in the water and some people think that because of this their skins are very slimy this is not so.

Instead write...

Amphibians include a number of different animals such as frogs, toads, and salamanders. They spend part of their lives on land and part of their lives in the water. Because of this, some people think their skins are very slimy, but this is not so.

- **Omitted or misspelled words**

Check each word carefully. It is easy to leave out an important word when you are writing quickly! If a word looks wrong, try spelling it another way.

Example
Amphains include a number of **diffrent** animals such as **frots**, toads, and **salimanders** that part of their lives on land and part of their lives in the water.

Instead write….

Amphibians include a number of **different** animals such as **frogs**, toads, and **salamanders** that **spend** part of their lives on land and part of their lives in the water.

- **Incorrect grammar**

Do your verbs agree with your subjects? Have you used pronouns correctly?

Example
Amphibians include a number of different animals such as frogs, toads, and salamanders that spends part of its life on land and part of its life in the water.

Instead write…

Amphibians include a number of different animals such as frogs, toads, and salamanders that **spend** part of **their lives** on land and part of **their lives** in the water.

- **Errors in punctuation**

Does every sentence have a question mark, period, or exclamation mark at the end? Are your commas in the right place? Are you using commas where periods should go?

Example
Amphibians are animals such as toads frogs, and salamanders that begin their lives in the water Later they develop lungs and live on the land

Instead write…

Amphibians are animals such as toads, frogs, and salamanders that begin their lives in the water. Later they develop lungs and live on the land.

Think About It!

Think about all the suggestions for taking tests from the last few pages.

Write down some of the strengths you already have as a test taker.

_____

_____

_____

_____

Write down three new ideas that you will try as you work to become a better test taker.

_____

_____

_____

These are suggestions that may help you do better on tests. These pages will probably help you most as references. You probably discovered that you already do many of the things. That's great!

Look for a few new ideas that you will try the next time you take a test.

Remember to read these pages again before you take an important test.

Using Rubrics

"I can do a great project for history this grading period," Brad confided to his sister Kaylee. "Usually when we have a project I have to guess how the teacher might grade it. However, this time our teacher gave us a rubric. It shows exactly what she thinks is important to include in the project and exactly how she will grade it. This is going to make it so much easier to do a good job."

In addition to tests and quizzes, another important tool for assessing student work is a **rubric**. Many teachers use rubrics to help guide students as they do projects (such as a model or collage) or performances (such as a skit or an oral report). Rubrics also assess writing assignments. Most rubrics have numbers or points included so that you can see how to score your product.

Rubrics have two important functions that will help you become an achiever. First, they have a list of criteria that helps you understand what is important to the teacher and what the teacher is looking for when he or she grades your work. Be sure to read and follow the rubric very carefully. Then you won't need to guess what the teacher wants. It is right in front of you in black and white!

Secondly, rubrics can serve as your guide as you are working. Reread the rubric often. See where you are in your work and how you need to improve your project before you turn it in. Most rubrics have several columns with descriptions in each block. Try to make your work match the best descriptor in the rubric. Students who are good at reading and following directions are usually good at reading and following rubrics!

Think About It!

Which of your teachers or classes often use rubrics?

_____

_____

In what ways have rubrics been helpful to you?

_____

_____

How can you use rubrics to improve your achievement in the future?

_____

_____

_____

An Achiever Rubric

Look at the rubric below. Where would you score today?
Try using this rubric often as you work to become an achiever.

Criteria:	Not So Hot	Working On It	Almost There	You're an Achiever
Self Confidence	I know I'll just be a failure so I don't even try.	I think I have some strengths, and I try not to get discouraged when I fail at something.	I learn from my failures. My parents and friends have confidence in me.	I know I will do well in anything I try. I look forward to learning from my mistakes and I never give up.
Goal Setting	I don't set any goals. I hope I'll be lucky and win the lottery one day.	I set goals for the week or grading period in at least one subject.	I have short-term and long-term goals and check regularly to see how I'm doing.	I set goals regularly and have a plan for meeting my goals. I plan backward for short and long- term goals.
Motivation	I don't care what happens to me in school or in the rest of my life.	I'm interested in learning a few things. I have to be motivated by others to get my work done.	I try very hard even when things are difficult. My friends and family encourage me. Sometimes I'm a bit lazy.	I have lots of interests and am excited about learning. I put forth the most effort when the task is difficult.
Organizational Skills	I am totally disorganized! I can't remember my assignments and I lose everything.	Sometimes I write down my assignments, and I get most things done although I procrastinate a lot.	I am organized, get all my homework done, but never have time to do things I enjoy.	My schoolwork, homework, and life outside of school are in order. I plan long-range assignments and have time to have fun, too.
Study Skills	I never study and really don't know how to begin.	Sometimes I study, but it's almost always at the last minute.	I get all my homework done. I know how to do a research paper and how to memorize things for a test.	I have excellent study skills. I know how to research, take notes, and memorize new information. I am always prepared for tests.

Assessment Using Portfolios

Ms. Knight is a wonderful math teacher. At the beginning of the school year, she assigned a file folder to each of her students. As the year went on, students put all of their work into their individual folders.

One day, Ms. Knight wrote the word PORTFOLIO on the board. She asked her students which activities they felt would show both their **effort** and **learning** in math. She wanted to know what they thought the most important things were.

Some said that the papers, which showed their best work, were most important. Others said it should be their worst work. Some kids picked the assignments they enjoyed the most, while others choose the assignments with the most challenging problems.

Together the class decided what should go into the portfolio. Each student was allowed to review his or her own portfolio and write an introduction about what was included in it and why. Each person spent time reading and grading the portfolios of other students. All of the students felt that having a portfolio was a good way for them to reflect about and see what they had learned.

Developing Portfolios

Sometimes schools use portfolios to assess students' work. Possibly you have developed one. There are many different ways to use portfolios. You might have wondered exactly what a portfolio is. One definition states that it is a collection of a student's work that tells the story of a student's efforts, progress, or achievement in school.

Portfolios show a lot more about what students know and what they can do than a multiple-choice test does. They show the process students go through in getting an answer or designing a project.

Unlike taking a test, the process of developing a portfolio usually allows you to correct the mistakes you make. It is more than just a folder with some of your work in it. It may contain the finished product of some work and the beginning stage of something else.

Sometimes teachers will tell you exactly what to put in your portfolio, but at other times you can decide for yourself and highlight your best work. Most of the time, students help decide what will be in the portfolio and how to judge it. Portfolios usually give you the opportunity to think about the work you have done and tell the teacher something about how the assignment was helpful, how you could improve, how it is related to something else you are doing, etc. It allows you to think about your growth and the changes you make over time.

Portfolios show both learning and effort, so it is fine to include some of the things that were hard for you and that you struggled with. Achievers usually show lots of effort and that they have learned a great deal, even when the final product is far from perfect! Portfolios are excellent tools for students who are becoming achievers. You may have forgotten how much you have learned and how much progress you have made in the course of a few months or a year. Your portfolio can show you your achievement and your progress.

Portfolios have many different uses. Use them with a college admissions application, as a way for you and your teacher to show your parents the work you've done, or to pass information on to the next teacher about your level of work, your strengths, and your weaknesses.

Make good use of any opportunity you may have to develop a portfolio. If you are given time to redo papers and correct mistakes, be sure to do it. Think about how you learn best—your learning style—and what the items in your portfolio tell you about how you learn. Portfolios can teach you to think about yourself, your strengths, and your abilities. Make sure you use them thoughtfully!

Think About It!

What types of work would you like to include in your portfolio?

_____

_____

_____

_____

Think of 5 of the most important assignments or projects you have done in the past six months. Write them below. What did you learn from each?

Project or Assignment   What I Learned

_____

_____

_____

_____

_____

7. Dealing with "The System"

"This school is so dumb," Eric grumbled. "Here I am in 9th grade, and they still treat me like a baby. I have to write the answers to questions I already know and read stories in a textbook that doesn't interest me at all. I have to get on the bus at 6:30 in the morning and then ride all around town before it finally gets to the school at 7:15. However, it should only be a ten-minute ride! There's something wrong with the school system!"

"I signed up for jazz band so I could play my sax, and now they tell me that class is filled and there's no room for me. So they're scheduling me for a childcare class. I don't want to take childcare!" Angie could barely control her anger. "Why is this school system so messed up? I feel like not doing any work, just as a protest. I'll show them!"

"Our class was supposed to go on a field trip to Sea World," said Coretta. "It was going to be so much fun. Even our teacher, Mr. Max, was excited. Then the school board came out with a policy that said no more field trips. It isn't fair! Why do they do things like that?"

Local School Systems

Eric, Angie, and Coretta all have problems with **"The System."** Maybe you have problems with **"The System,"** too. Lots of kids do. The school system refers to the institution that has been set up and given the authority to run the schools within a certain area. In order to deal effectively with the system and make it work for you, you need to understand how it is organized and how it operates. There's more to it than you probably have imagined!

School, like the government, the military, business, and industry, is a "system." You may have heard your school district referred to as the "school system." All systems have rules and regulations that everyone has to follow in order for the system to run smoothly for the **majority** of its people. These rules make the organization run smoothly. Unfortunately, sometimes these rules seem pretty senseless, and some students don't understand why they have to follow them.

In the United States, the majority of our schools are run **locally.** Each county, city, or town can have its own school system. This is different from many other countries in the world where the national government runs the schools. Because schools are run locally, we have many, many school systems, or school districts. Some school districts are very big with thousands of employees and hundreds of schools. Others may be quite small. In fact, in some school districts there are only two or three schools in the whole district! In most schools **the school board** is a group of elected people who operate the school district. They work with the **superintendent of schools**, a person who is in charge of running the school district on a day-to-day basis. In a large school district, there are many other superintendents known as **assistant** or **associate superintendents**. Each school has a leader called the **principal**, and many schools have other people in leadership positions such as an **assistant principal** or **dean of students**.

Each state has a **Department of Education** that makes policies that all schools in the state must follow. The state legislature passes laws governing the schools, including how much money school districts receive.

The national government in Washington, D.C. also has policies that affect your local school system. There also are some national laws and some court orders from the Supreme Court that affect how the schools function and the amount of money they receive.

As you can see, there is a lot of **bureaucracy** to sift through when you deal with the school system! It is important to know whether something is a local, state, or national policy if you decide to work with the system to bring about change. Remember that bureaucracies require going through the "proper channels" so don't get discouraged or confused as you try to understand how the system works.

Think About It!

What is your school system like?

_____

_____

_____

Who is in charge?

_____

How large a system is it? _____

In the space below, describe your school system. If you do not know about it, find out!

_____

_____

_____

_____

_____

_____

Bringing About Change

Believe it or not, school systems can be changed! In fact, one of the things schools are most interested in is finding ways to change and improve so that they can better serve students! School **reform** or **school restructuring** is the term for the change, and there are many different ideas about how the schools should reform.

Some schools in the same school district may have different rules, structures, or policies about how they select students. For example, charter schools can often experiment with new ways to do things. If you want a school that is open to change, many charter schools are good places to look!

A magnet school is another type of school generally open to change. These schools have a very specific focus or emphasis. For instance, there might be a magnet school for technology and another one for arts or foreign languages.

Public schools have to follow many federal and state laws. Sometimes it is very hard for them to change. Private and parochial (religious) schools don't have to follow as many government rules and regulations as public schools do, but often they have rules and regulations of their own!

You need to know something about the laws and rules your school operates under before you can decide on realistic ways to change it.

Think About It!

This is the way our school operates:

People in charge _____

_____

_____

General rules for everyone in our school

_____

_____

Rules in my classroom(s)

_____

_____

_____

One way to change things at your school or in your school district is to talk to your parents about it, and ask them to help you. As strange as it may seem, you and your parents have lots of power with the school system! Most school boards and superintendents want to hear the ideas parents have about making schools better. Parents with good ideas can work through the PTA, their school principal, the school advisory council, or just as individuals to communicate those ideas in a positive way to the school board and superintendent.

Challenging and Changing "The System"

It is okay to challenge the system, but if you want to change something, you must have a game plan much like your own academic game plan. No change occurs if you are only a complainer and point out what's wrong. On the other hand, it is helpful if you see a way to change "the system" for the better. Think about a plan for change and then present it to someone in charge. Identify the person or group of people who have the authority to make the change you want. This may be a teacher, department head, grade level chairperson, the principal, the school board, or the superintendent of schools.

Sometimes **how** you ask is more important than **what** you're asking for. The principal, people on the school board, or those in the state department of education don't want to know how boring you think school is. They don't want to know that you think "the system" stinks or that you hate your chemistry teacher! But they are interested in improving education for all students and will appreciate your ideas about how to change things for the better — ways to make school more interesting and subjects more challenging.

An organization that is set up to give students a voice in what goes on in their school is the **student government** or **student council.** Find out how you can become an active member of this organization at your school. Work with the organization to bring about the changes you want.

Think About It!

What do you want out of school? What do you wish to change? On a separate pieces of paper, write down what you truly want out of school. Think about your goals for the future as you write.

What changes would you like in your school or school system?

_____

_____

*Think about how you could help make these changes!
Write a letter or email someone in authority explaining your point of view.

The Importance of Humor

Have you ever noticed that schools are pretty funny places? Funny things go on in schools every day! When you get frustrated by the system or angry with a teacher, keep your positive sense of humor! This relieves stress and gives you a good perspective for the long haul.

Achievers are serious about their goals, but most achievers don't take themselves too seriously. They learn to "roll with the punches," enjoy learning, and appreciate life. Maintaining a good sense of humor is one of the greatest gifts you can give to yourself as you go through life. Laughter is good for the soul. Make a habit of it!

Final Thoughts

Congratulations! You've made it all the way to the end of this book. I hope that you have learned a lot by reading it and that you are ready to work on all of the steps to Become an Achiever.

This book was not written to be read once and then become a dust collector on a shelf. Much of what it contains will encourage you to think about your own life: your self-confidence, your goals, your motivation, your ability to organize yourself, and to manage time and study. As you grow, you will change. What motivates you in 5th grade will not be what motivates you in 10th grade.

Review this book from time to time to see how you've changed. Each time you read it, you will get new ideas and new insights about yourself. Continue to do your best as you follow the steps to Become an Achiever!

**WE MUST BECOME
THE CHANGE
WE WANT TO SEE**

MAHATMA GANDHI

Activity Books to use as you Become an Achiever . . .

Below are some selected books from Pieces of Learning. For more information or to order them, call 1-800-729-5137 or visit our web site at www.piecesoflearning.com

Writing and Language Arts
You're the Teacher: Editing for Kids (CD's)
Writing with Character
Writing: one day at a time
You Choose
Poetry Patterns
Playwright
Word Play

Math
Math Rules! series
Math in History

Social Studies
State by State
Historical Hoaxes

Science
Critters and Bugs of Africa
Critters and Bugs of The Great Sonoran Desert
Critters and Bugs of The Tropical Rainforest

Research and Independent Study
Let Your Fingers Do the Searching
How to Write the Best Research Paper Ever
Independent Study
Research Reports to Knock Your Teacher's Socks Off
Research Without Copying
Extra Credit

Thinking Skills and Creativity
Creativity Calendar
Jestercises and Gamestorms
Quick Question Workbook
Spurs to Creative Thinking
Look Closer: Visual Thinking Skills